6/9/10 cf

8/12

15 APR 2013

12 JUN 2013
15 MAY 2014
27 JUN 2014

WEST MOORS
MOBILE

AMB.CH
LTANF
ACR.CSD
CAR.CSJ

HOME LIBRARY MOBILE
CENTRAL DIVISION
DORCHESTER
TEL 01305 224446

WL
SX
LS
Z

Dorchester Mobile
Dorchester
01305 224089

FH 17

Dorset Libraries
Withdrawn Stock

- Please return items before closing time on the last date stamped to avoid charges.
- Renew books by phoning 01305 224311 or online www.dorsetforyou.com/libraries
- Items may be returned to any Dorset library.
- Please note that children's books issued on an adult card will incur overdue charges.

Dorset County Council
Library Service

DL/2372 dd05450

D1336900

DORSET COUNTY LIBRARY

205261563 U

When FOOTBALL *Was* FOOTBALL

WORLD CUP

© Haynes Publishing, 2010

The right of Adam Powley to be identified as the author of this Work has been asserted
by him in accordance with the Copyright, Designs & Patents Act 1988.

All rights reserved. No part of this publication may be reproduced, stored in a retrieval system
or transmitted, in any form or by any means, electronic, mechanical, photocopying, recording
or otherwise, without prior permission in writing from the publisher.

First published in 2010

A catalogue record for this book is available from the British Library

ISBN: 978-1-844259-62-5

Published by Haynes Publishing, Sparkford, Yeovil,
Somerset BA22 7JJ, UK
Tel: 01963 442030 Fax: 01963 440001
Int. tel: +44 1963 442030 Int. fax: +44 1963 440001
E-mail: sales@haynes.co.uk
Website: www.haynes.co.uk

Haynes North America Inc., 861 Lawrence Drive,
Newbury Park, California 91320, USA

All images © Mirrorpix

Creative Director: Kevin Gardner
Packaged for Haynes by BrainWave

Printed and bound in the US

When
FOOTBALL *Was*
FOOTBALL

WORLD CUP

A Nostalgic Look at Football's Greatest Competition

Dorset County Library		
Askews	2010	
796.334668	£18.99	

Adam Powley

Contents

Introduction

The World Cup – the greatest show on Earth. The Olympics may claim to be the biggest multi-sport extravaganza, and sports like cricket and rugby may grab the headlines every four years or so, but as a single event that captures the imagination of virtually the whole planet, the football World Cup has no equal.

Born in the aftermath of World War, it grew from a somewhat off-the-cuff get together to become the slick multi-billion dollar phenomenon it is today. The World Cup has a power to unite whole nations, transcending politics, race, gender and age. When the World Cup whistle blows, the world comes to a standstill.

The sadness is that the modern World Cup's all-conquering success has stripped away some of its former appeal. Combine wall-to-wall media coverage with the globalization of the game, throw the Champions League and computer games into the mix, and fans are left with a tournament that holds few surprises. We all know almost everything there is to know about teams and players. Whereas footballers from South America used to be an exotic curiosity, they are now all-too familiar. There's no mystery any more – and mystery is partly what made the World Cup so special.

The people's game... Vast crowds have been an inherent feature of the World Cup, as with this joyous celebration in central London after England's famous 1966 triumph.

This book celebrates the time when the World Cup was *really* special. It harks back to a different age, when footballers played for the pride of representing their country, not the opportunity to parade themselves and land a lucrative move to a big club or attract sponsors. It's about the great games, the legendary players, the colour, character and excitement of tournaments from the past – not the commercialized, sanitized, marketed 'football experience' that the tournament has become.

For that reason, our story ends with the 1994 World Cup. That is not to say that subsequent tournaments have not provided thrilling football, nor that the competitions of the 'good old days' were all sporting sweetness and light free of the less-savoury aspects of the game. It's simply that the World Cup was different in the past.

This is a story not just about the famous events on the pitch. It's also about the moments away from the game, the World Cup behind the scenes: Brazil's Gilmar on a shopping trip in Manchester, England players mixing with the locals in Mexico, the tales of the fans who travelled far and wide to support their team.

To paraphrase Pelé's oft-repeated quote about football, this book is about the World Cup when it was a more beautiful game; when the World Cup was the World Cup – and football really was football.

Adam Powley

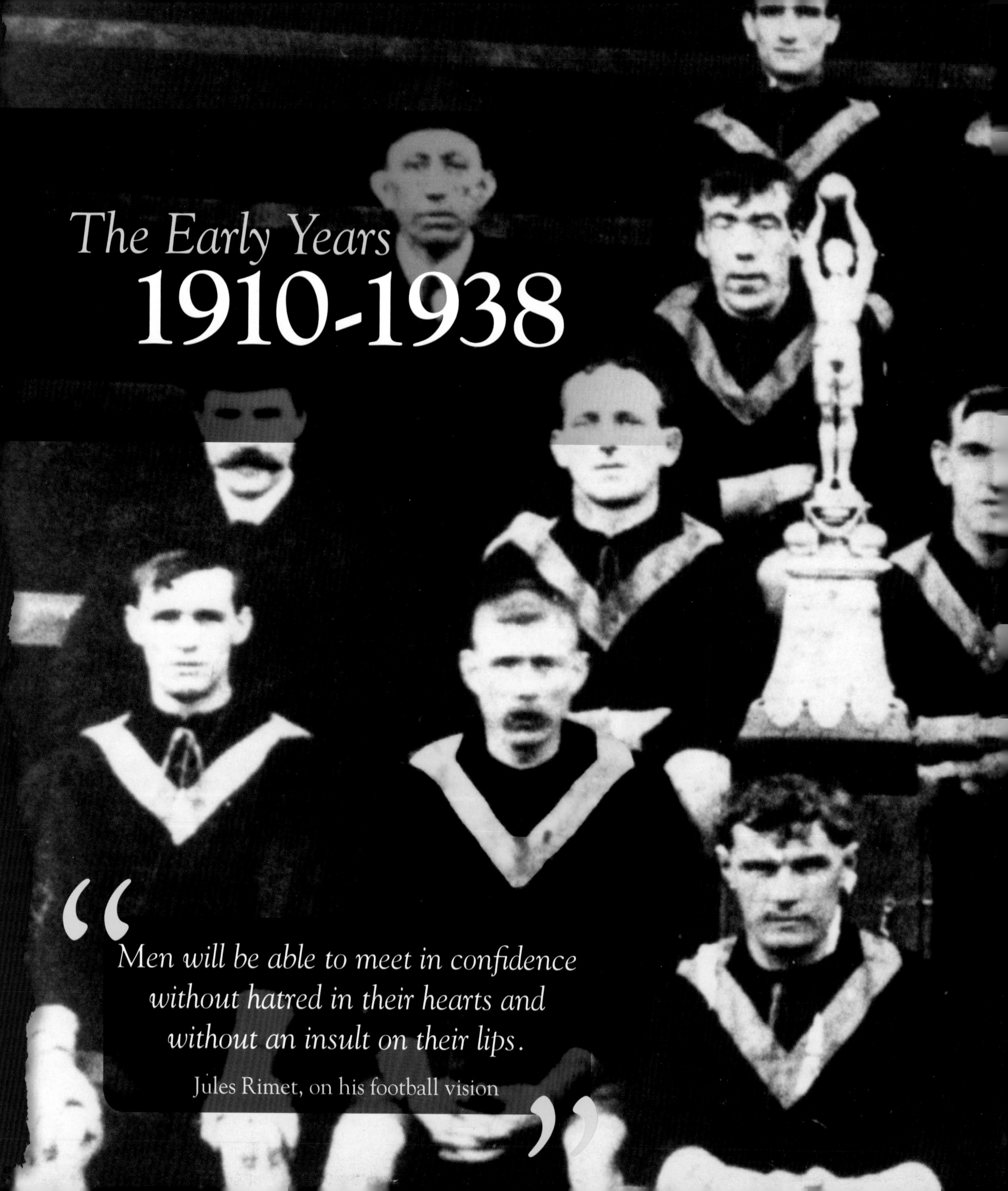

The Early Years
1910-1938

"

*Men will be able to meet in confidence
without hatred in their hearts and
without an insult on their lips.*

Jules Rimet, on his football vision

"

When
FOOTBALL *Was*
FOOTBALL

The year is 1911 and the first "world cup" comes home for good to the country that gave the world the modern game. The victors were not England or any of the other home nations but West Auckland Town, a team of Durham miners who twice took on Europe's biggest club sides and won. The tournament was organized by the tea baron Sir Thomas Lipton, by way of a thank-you for being awarded the Grand Order of Italy. How West Auckland ended up representing England is a matter of some debate. One story is that Lipton approached the Football League to invite one of its club sides to take part, but the League refused – a sign of things to come for nearly 50 years of English isolationism. Lipton turned instead to West Auckland, having supposedly been impressed by a letter from a youngster who lived in the pit village.

After defeating Stuttgart and Swiss side FC Winterthur in Turin, West Auckland won the competition in 1909 and secured it again two years later by beating FC Zurich and thrashing Juventus 6-1.

West Auckland's exploits were dramatized in 1982 in the TV film *A Captain's Tale* starring Dennis Waterman as skipper Bob Jones.

In 1904, the Fédération Internationale de Football Association (FIFA) was formed by six original members: France, Germany, the Netherlands, Belgium, Denmark and Switzerland. FIFA's Antwerp conference in 1920 first proposed the idea of a competition between national sides, instigated by its new president, Jules Rimet; in the same year British teams withdrew from FIFA amid political disputes left over from the First World War and a wider hostility towards other nations controlling what the home nations perceived as "their" game. The first World Cup was eventually held in 1930 in Uruguay, with 13 nations taking part. Qualifying entailed four groups, one of four teams the rest of three each; France only decided in April to attend and make the three-week journey by sea. The match between France and Argentina on 15th July almost ended in farce when the referee blew for time six minutes early, but restarted the game to complete the allotted time. Uruguay eventually won the tournament on 30th July, beating Argentina 4-2 with their fourth goal scored by one-armed striker Hector Castro. For the 1934 tournament in Italy, a straight knockout format was introduced. Holders Uruguay refused to take part in retaliation for the snubs of various European nations four years earlier, and because of a players' strike. After defeating the much fancied Austrians and their star performer Matthias Sindelar on 3rd June, the hosts defeated Czechoslovakia 2-1 after extra time in Rome, becoming the first European side to win the Jules Rimet. **Four years later,** Italy became the first country to retain the trophy. Spain were absent due to the civil war, Austria merged with the German side after its annexation to Germany on 12th March 1938, Brazil displayed the free-flowing football for which they were to become famous, while British teams again remained at home.

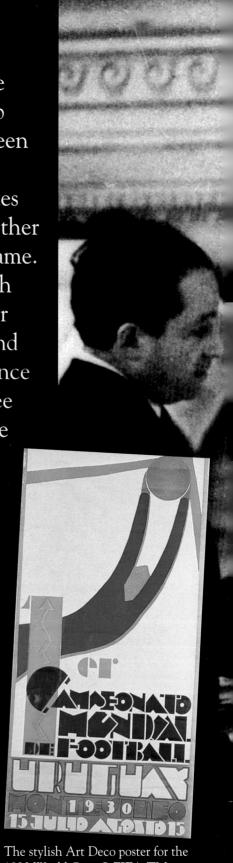

The stylish Art Deco poster for the 1930 World Cup © **FIFA TM**

As with the 1936 German Olympics, the 1934 World Cup was a prime example of how sport could be exploited for political purposes by totalitarian regimes. Italy's leader Benito Mussolini (below, in discussion with the chief of his newspaper service), was determined to use the tournament to showcase the power of fascist society: no expense was spared to ensure the tournament was held in Italy; the hosts fielded four *oriundi*, foreign players qualified through their Italian parentage and thus deprived Argentina of some of their best talents – Orsi, Monti, De Maria and Guaita; some of the officiating was notably generous to the home side; and there was even a trophy specially commissioned by Mussolini to be presented alongside the Jules Rimet. The Coppa Del Duce dwarfed its counterpart, and will be remembered only as a tasteless and vulgar symbol of Il Duce's ego and vanity.

FIELD FOR COMPARISONS

Miss Hartigan is playing at Beckenham, but Mrs. Sperling is uncertain. The Wightman Cup "discards"—Miss Stammers, Mrs. Pittman, Miss Heeley and others—are in the field, too, and if any of them should strike the form they are capable of, and things do not go too smoothly for the British team at Wimbledon, there will be the inevitable comparisons.

Mrs. Pittman won her third women's singles final in succession at the St. George's Hill tournament at Weybridge, where she beat Miss R. M. Hardwick 6—4, 3—6, 6—3.

I thought Mrs. Pittman played as though she had had enough tennis for a little while. There was an absence of sparkle about the game, and Miss Hardwick did not move fast enough to turn numerous chances to account.

Fulham's new manager, Mr. James Hogan, believes in keeping himself in strict training. Here is Mr. Hogan (centre) with his son (light shirt) running round the Fulham track.

The World Cup final receives only the most cursory of mentions in the *Daily Mirror* on 11th June 1934. The lack of media coverage reflected the insularity of the British football establishment. Up to the 1950s, whole tournaments would be completed without any detailed reports or news; results would be relegated to brief paragraphs, tucked away at the bottom of pages. Even then, the description "world" was placed in quotation marks, suggesting newspaper editors scoffed at the idea the tournament even deserved the description.

NEUSEL TO MEET SCHMELING

ITALY'S SOCCER HONOUR

Italy won the "World" Football Championship in Rome yesterday by defeating Czechoslovakia 2—1 after extra time.

> *We played for the cup, leaving aside all flourishes.*
>
> Italy's two-time World Cup-winning coach, Vittorio Pozzo

In the post-war era, British sides came in from the cold to compete against footballing nations beyond their shores. Leaving for the exotic climes of Rio de Janeiro for the 1950 tournament, England's Stan Mortensen (left) and Billy Wright cast an admiring eye over air hostess Neuza De Almeida.

Taking to the White Hart Lane field for a tussle with World Cup holders Italy on 30th November 1949, England won 2-0.

Between **1939** and **1945**, while war raged across the globe, FIFA vice-president Dr Ottorino Barassi kept the World Cup trophy safe under his bed. When the conflict ended the cup was formally named the Jules Rimet trophy. In **1946** British teams were finally readmitted into the FIFA fold. Work began on the massive Maracanã Stadium in **1948**. The Superga plane crash disaster of **1949** that wiped out the great Torino side also decimated the Italian squad, which featured a number of Torino players. Scotland declined an invitation to compete in the **1950** finals as they had not finished top of the British home internationals qualifying group. For the first (and only) time, the World Cup was decided on a round-robin final group basis; Uruguay were the shock winners over hosts Brazil. **1952** saw Hungary win the Olympic title, following it up with a 6-3 humbling of England a year later that confirmed their status as the world's best side and red-hot favourites to lift the **1954** World Cup crown. Scotland made their World Cup debut on **16**th **June 1954**, losing 1-0 to Austria before succumbing to a 7-0 thrashing by Uruguay. **4**th **July 1954** became forever known in Germany as the day of the "Miracle of Berne" when West Germany came from two goals down to beat the mighty Hungarians. The tournament ended with 140 goals in 26 matches, a World Cup record. For the **1958** finals, the Soviet Union qualified for the first time; for the first and only time to date, all four British home nations also took part; on **17**th **June** Northern Ireland defeated Czechoslovakia, to move into the quarter-finals. Two days earlier, a 17-year-old Pelé made his World Cup debut in the 2-0 Group 4 win over the Soviet Union. On **29**th **June** he scored for Brazil in their 5-2 win in the final against hosts Sweden. Chile, host nation for the 1962 finals, was struck by a massive earthquake in **May 1960**, yet was able to stage the finals due to an astonishing rebuilding effort. **2**nd **June 1962** was the day of the violent "Battle of Santiago" clash between Chile and Italy. In beating Czechoslovakia 3-1 on **17**th **June**, Brazil retained the World Cup trophy.

Walter Winterbottom (wearing glasses) was in confident mood before departing for South America in 1950. England's first orthodox manager (teams had previously been picked by the FA committee), he reigned for 16 years and took the national side to four World Cups, despite the humiliation of being in charge for the infamous 1-0 defeat to the USA in England's second World Cup finals match. Several British newspapers thought the reported score line was a mistake and printed it as "10-1" to England.

The gigantic Maracanã Stadium in Rio de Janeiro became a three-tiered monument to Brazil's footballing passion. A crowd of 199,854 packed in for the 1950 final game against Uruguay.

JOHN THOMPSON'S first cable from Rio

THEY'RE GOING 'NUTS' ON SOCCER IN BRAZIL

Forbes puts club before Bogota trip

Festival Tour

Wives Are Barred

Vitamin Nightcaps

Beautiful Girls

F.A. 'NO' TO FLOODLIT PLAY MAY PROVE TO BE UNWISE

Brazil's 'victory' cup song became a silent samba

So certain were the Brazilians of winning the World Soccer Cup that they wrote and recorded a samba—"Brazil the Victors." But now it will probably become known as the "Silent Samba." For Brazil, red-hot favourites, were beaten 2–1 by Uruguay in Rio de Janeiro last night.

The 200,000 Brazilians who paid a world record of £125,000 to watch the game, were thunderstruck as Uruguay became new world champions. Many women in the huge blue and white stadium were prostrate with grief and others wept openly.

The whole city was plunged in gloom, and stadium doctors said they treated 169 people for fits of hysteria and other troubles. Six fans were taken to hospital seriously ill.

ABOVE: *Mirror* reporters cabled some exotic despatches.

MULLEN SIGNS
Jimmy Mullen, Wolves' winger who helped England beat Chile 2–0 in the World Cup in Rio on Sunday, gives his autograph to a Brazilian girl fan.

ABOVE: With British teams now enthusiastic guests at the World Cup party, sports journalists were at last free to report on proceedings in some detail and colour. The *Mirror*'s indefatigable John Thompson posted a colourful piece from Rio – and proved to be a shrewd judge in criticizing the FA's decision not to allow England to play at night: the daytime heat was to prove costly to their campaign.

1954

Hungary, the "Magical Magyars", went into the 1954 finals as the team everybody wanted to see. Their revolutionary tactical approach, allied to a line-up blessed with ball-playing artists, was way ahead of their competitors. They were led by the great Ferenc Puskás as the team's fulcrum. The "Galloping Major" attended a Hungarian Sports Exhibition in London just after his side had humiliated an England side that was stuck in a tactical and technical time warp by comparison. And yet Hungary fell at the final hurdle in 1954, beaten by a comparatively inferior West German side making its first appearance in the finals since the war.

LEFT: Puskás in later (and more rotund) times.

The British home nations and the paying public were at least now taking the World Cup seriously, as in this qualifying meeting between Wales and England in front of a packed Ninian Park in 1953.

Key to the World Cup series

By BOB FERRIER

FROM thirty-three nations who took part in the qualifying competition, the top sixteen, the world's greatest football teams, contest the final stages of the World Championships in Switzerland, starting this week, with the final in Berne on July 4.

The sixteen have been split up into four groups of four, with two "seeded" teams in each group. The seeded teams do NOT play each other.

After the first round, two teams go forward to quarter-finals on a points basis.

Draw for the first round is:

Group I.—*Brazil v. Mexico (Geneva, June 16); Brazil v. Yugoslavia (Lausanne, June 19); *France v. Yugoslavia (Lausanne, June 16); France v. Mexico (Geneva, June 19).

Group II.—*Hungary v. Korea (Zurich, June 17); Hungary v. Germany (Basle, June 20); *Turkey v. Korea (Geneva, June 20); Turkey v. Germany (Berne, June 17).

Group III.—*Austria v. Scotland (Zurich, June 16); Austria v. Czechoslovakia (Zurich, June 19); *Uruguay v. Scotland (Basle, June 19); Uruguay v. Czechoslovakia (Berne, June 16).

Group IV.—*England v. Belgium (Basle, June 17); England v. Switzerland (Berne, June 20); *Italy v. Belgium (Lugano, June 20); Italy v. Switzerland (Lausanne, June 17).

* Seeded team.

The quarter-final draw will be divided into top (Groups I and II) and bottom (Groups II and III) sections. For instance, if Austria, Uruguay, England and Italy emerge from the first round, England would play one match against either Austria or Uruguay, with Italy playing the other.

If the semi-finalists emerge as England and Italy, for instance, each would play one match against one of the two semi-finalists from the top half.

The *Daily Mirror's* "World Cup wall chart" – of sorts – made its debut for the 1954 tournament.

Tommy Docherty in action for Scotland. Making their second consecutive appearance in the finals in 1958, the side again struggled, hindered by the curious reluctance of the Scottish management to field the likes of Dave Mackay, for example, who only played one qualifying game. Matt Busby had been due to manage the team, but was unable to do so after being injured in the Munich air disaster.

RIGHT: Mix young Latin footballers with ardent young Swedish admirers and what do you get? A "teenage riot" according to the *Daily Mirror* in June 1958.

TEENAGERS IN RIOT

ARGENTINA'S Soccer bosses yesterday angrily denied charges that there had been "fraternising" among some of their World Cup team with Swedish teenage girls.

A few hours earlier police were called out to calm down twenty-four girls who tried to force their way into the team's training camp.

1958

In their only appearance in a World Cup tournament to date, Wales gave a performance of much distinction. Managed by Jimmy Murphy and with the likes of Cliff Jones, Ivor Allchurch and the great John Charles (below, back row far right) in their ranks, they won through a tricky qualifying group that included Sweden and Hungary to reach the quarter-finals, only going out after a plucky 1-0 defeat to the eventual winners, Brazil, for whom Pelé scored the winner.

Mirror SPORT

It's a great night for the Welsh and Irish—they're in quarter-finals!

WORLD CUP SPECIAL

ENGLAND GO DOWN AND OUT

● Anxious moment for England as the ball slips beneath goalkeeper McDonald's body with Russia's Valentin Ivanov close by in the World Cup last night.

From BILL HOLDEN, Gothenburg, Tuesday

ENGLAND are out of the World Cup—and they can't complain.

All the energy they could dredge from their limbs and all the courage they could pull from their pounding hearts was not enough in this play-off against Russia here tonight.

The Russians, in this third meeting of the two countries in a month, were the masters in skill and science.

England were cheered off the pitch at the end before the crowd rose to give the Russians a much less enthusiastic send-off.

Russia were first to move into a threatening attack. But Apukhtin tamely flicked the ball yards outside the post.

Punched Clear

England first came near to scoring in the fifteenth minute, but from a free kick Yashin punched clear from centre forward Derek Kevan's blond head.

Goalkeeper McDonald, so often the hero here, saved England when he plunged to pluck the ball from the feet of inside right Ivanov.

But the Russian star came through twice more. Once he hit the side net, and then centre half Billy Wright stopped him after he had twinkled past three men.

Navvies

Compared with the Soccer science being served up by the Russians, the England team looked ham-handed navvies in hob-nailed boots.

Not until the thirty-seventh minute did Peter Broadbent, England's new inside right from Wolves, fire in the first shot for England, but it was a long one which Yashin had no trouble covering.

Broadbent was the best man of an unhappy England. He almost produced a goal with a cross from the right wing which Peter Brabrook, another new cap, got a foot to, but could only scoop into Yashin's clutch.

There was so little excitement in the stadium that I could clearly hear Billy Wright shouting: "Leave it, I want you in the middle," as Kevan tried to take a throw-in.

A new England opened the second half and within seven minutes Brabrook twice hit the foot of the same upright.

Next Brabrook bulldozed into range and cannoned a shot into the net, only to suffer supreme torment when he realised that this third great effort had been disallowed because he had handled.

THEN DISASTER STRUCK.

From Volnov's pass Ilyin crashed the ball in off the post, to put England a goal down after 69 minutes.

Kevan almost equalised with a brilliant burst but Yashin swooped down to take his shot in a steel trap hold.

Last Hope

There was hope once more when England were given a free kick on the edge of the penalty box because Referee Dusch thought the goalkeeper was guilty of time-wasting.

Slater took it and every England forward became a battering ram in an effort to get the ball home, but the wall of Russians foiled them.

ENGLAND.—McDonald; Howe, Banks; Clayton, Wright, Slater; Brabrook, Broadbent, Kevan, Haynes, A'Court. RUSSIA.—Yashin; Kesarov, Kuznetsov; Voinov, Krichevsky, Tsarev; Apukhtin, v Ivanov, Simonyan, Falin, Ilyin.

ENGLAND	-	-	-	-	-	-	0
RUSSIA	-	-	-	-	-	-	1

Ilyin, 69m.   H.T. 0—0.

Irish win in extra time

From JACK MILLIGAN

Ireland 2, Czechoslovakia 1 (after extra time)

Malmo, Tuesday

IRELAND, after a nervous start, fought back in this play-off after being a goal down in nineteen minutes and were level at half-time.

They were without Harry Gregg, their goalkeeper here of the previous games and centre forward Tom Casey.

Norman Uprichard (Portsmouth) and Jack Scott (Grimsby) deputised.

The Czechs went into the lead with a goal by right-winger Zikan after a free kick from Novak drifted into the penalty area.

Ireland's defenders stopped in their tracks expecting referee Guigue to award a free kick for a foul on Keith. He didn't and Zikan easily headed the ball over Uprichard's head.

Then after terrific Irish pressure Peter McParland, who moved to centre forward, thumped in a lovely pass from Cush to equalise fifty seconds from half-time.

Uprichard came out limping in the second half with an ankle injury, but was hardly troubled as Ireland rushed into the attack.

The Czechs panicked, and Bingham hit the bar with a header.

They rallied towards the end but were unable to pierce the Irish defence—and the game went into extra time.

After seven minutes of extra time McParland hit Ireland's winner, and as the game got rough Bubernik, Czech right half, was sent off after a vicious tackle.

Ireland now meet France in the Quarter Finals.

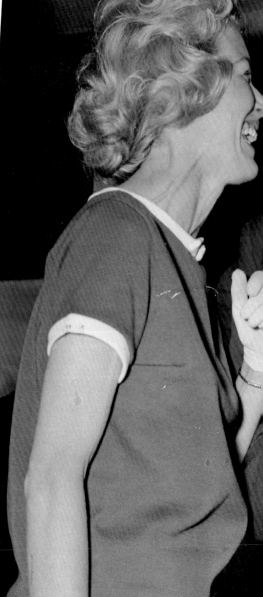

LEFT: England were sent packing after an unlucky 1-0 defeat to the Soviet Union in a Group 4 playoff in 1958. Twenty-year-old Bobby Charlton, returning to England (below left) did not even get on the pitch during the side's three matches, but his absence was perhaps understandable given his tender age and the fact that he had been injured in the Munich air disaster just four months earlier. The tragedy had shorn England of key players Duncan Edwards, Roger Byrne and Tommy Taylor.

BELOW: Also returning to London was skipper Billy Wright, welcomed by future wife Joy Beverley and accompanied by her singing sisters. Wright's World Cup record – he never played beyond the quarter-final in three tournaments – was scant reward for one of the country's most loyal and able footballing servants.

Top scorer at the 1958 finals was France's Just Fontaine with a record of 13 goals that still stands today. In 1978, Fontaine received his Golden Boot trophy.

The World Cup winners

THE MAN FROM THE MIRROR WAS THERE

Mirror **SPORT**

BRAZIL LICKED 'EM ALL—EXCEPT US!

From **BILL HOLDEN**
Stockholm, Sunday.

THE tiny golden trophy called the World Cup belongs to Brazil, who have won every match they have played in the competition except one —AGAINST ENGLAND.

They beat Sweden in the final here today, with startling simplicity. A game that should have been the supreme Soccer entertainment became an almost boring formality in the second half.

The brilliant, bewildering football masters of Brazil had mesmerised the Swedes into abject submission.

When it was over and president of F.I.F.A., England's Arthur Drewry had presented the cup, the South American officials told me:

"This game did not

SWEDEN . 2
BRAZIL . . 5
(H.T.: Sweden 1, Brazil 2)

worry us. The most difficult one of all, and the best football, was the match against England."

Brazil and England played out a goalless draw in one of the qualifying group matches which will live in my memory.

So Easy

It would have graced this stadium far more than the final which Brazil won so delightfully . . . BUT SO EASILY.

It began with football fit for the gods in the opening fifteen minutes. Swedish skipper Nils Liedholm danced through a closing

ring of defenders in the fourth minute.

It seemed odds on the inside left passing the ball to his unmarked centre forward, Agne Simonsson.

Instead, Liedholm swung his own lethal right foot, and flashed the ball into the far corner with goalkeeper Gylmar groping the air.

But the Brazilians refused to be upset by anything, and the Swedish rhapsody lasted only five minutes.

Then, right wing genius Garrincha, slickered through the defence and slipped the ball across perfectly for centre forward Vava to side foot it home.

Sewn Up

In the thirty-second minute Vava scored an identical goal and ten minutes after the interval the game was sewn up. Seventeen-year-old inside

left Pele swerved past three men in the way a matador evades a charging bull, and cracked the ball in.

Thirteen fatal minutes later outside left Zagalio made it 4—1.

Brazil were toying with the Swedes—playing out time—when two had decisions by French referee Maurice Gigue at last livened things up.

Slithered

As Garrincha slithered through the defence once again, a Swede desperately pulled him back by the arm.

It was inside the area, but the referee turned down penalty appeals and gave a free-kick on the edge of the box.

Only two minutes later Simonsson scored from an obviously offside position.

Then Pele headed in Brazil's fifth goal from Zagalio's cross in the last second.

For the first time a SOUTH AMERICAN team had won the World Cup on a EUROPEAN ground— and how they celebrated!

They are still letting off fireworks, and firing blank cartridge pistols as I phone this story.

All that is left for us, is the memory that the one team those tremendous Soccer masters could not beat was—ENGLAND.

● The jubilant Brazilian footballers grab a huge flag from Swedish supporters and carry it in triumph round the pitch after winning the World Cup final.

The *Mirror* paid tribute to the excellence of 1958 winners Brazil and their 17-year-old prodigy Pelé (but could not resist a spirited reference to England's otherwise undistinguished campaign).

19

1962

World Cup 1962 — FIXTURES AND SCORE CHART

	GROUP ONE (at Arica)		GROUP TWO (at Santiago)		GROUP THREE (at Viña del Mar)		GROUP FOUR (at Rancagua)	
DATE								
May 30	Uruguay	v. Colombia	Chile	v. Switzerland .	Brazil	v. Mexico	Argentina	v. Bulgaria ......
May 31	U.S.S.R.	v. Yugoslavia .	W. Germany	v. Italy	Spain	v. Czechoslovakia	ENGLAND	v. Hungary ......
June 2	Uruguay	v. Yugoslavia .	Chile	v. Italy	Brazil	v. Czechoslovakia	ENGLAND	v. Argentina ......
June 3	Colombia	v. U.S.S.R.	Switzerland	v. W. Germany	Mexico	v. Spain	Bulgaria	v. Hungary ......
June 6	Uruguay	v. U.S.S.R.	Chile	v. W. Germany	Brazil	v. Spain	Argentina	v. Hungary ......
June 7	Colombia	v. Yugoslavia .	Switzerland	v. Italy	Mexico	v. Czechoslovakia	ENGLAND	v. Bulgaria ......

TABLE	W	D	L	Pts		TABLE	W	D	L	Pts		TABLE	W	D	L	Pts		TABLE	W	D	L	Pts
1st						1st						1st						1st				
2nd						2nd						2nd						2nd				
3rd						3rd						3rd						3rd				
4th						4th						4th						4th				

QUARTER FINALS—JUNE 10

Match 1—winners of Group 1 play runners-up in Group 2
Match 2—winners of Group 2 play runners-up in Group 1
Match 3—winners of Group 3 play runners-up in Group 4
Match 4—winners of Group 4 play runners-up in Group 3

Match 1 Result	Match 2 Result	Match 3 Result	Match 4 Result
........v........	........v........	........v........	........v........

SEMI-FINALS—JUNE 13

(at Santiago)   (at Viña del Mar)

........v........   ....v........
(Match 1 wnr) (Match 3 wnr)   (Match 2 wnr) (Match 4 wnr)

(The match for third and fourth places, between the losers of the two semi-finals, will be played at Santiago on June 16)

........v........

THE WORLD FINAL—JUNE 17

........v........

KEEP FOR YOUR COMPLETE WORLD CUP RECORD.

Thumbs up and smiles as the England party set off for South America: it included Jimmy Greaves, Bobby Robson, Johnny Haynes and Jimmy Armfield.

The 1962 tournament marked a change in tactical emphasis towards more defensive approaches. The goals-per-game average dropped below three for the first time (and is yet to recover since), compared with 5.4 in 1954.

Walter Winterbottom checking baggage before departure.

England's Finest Hour 1966

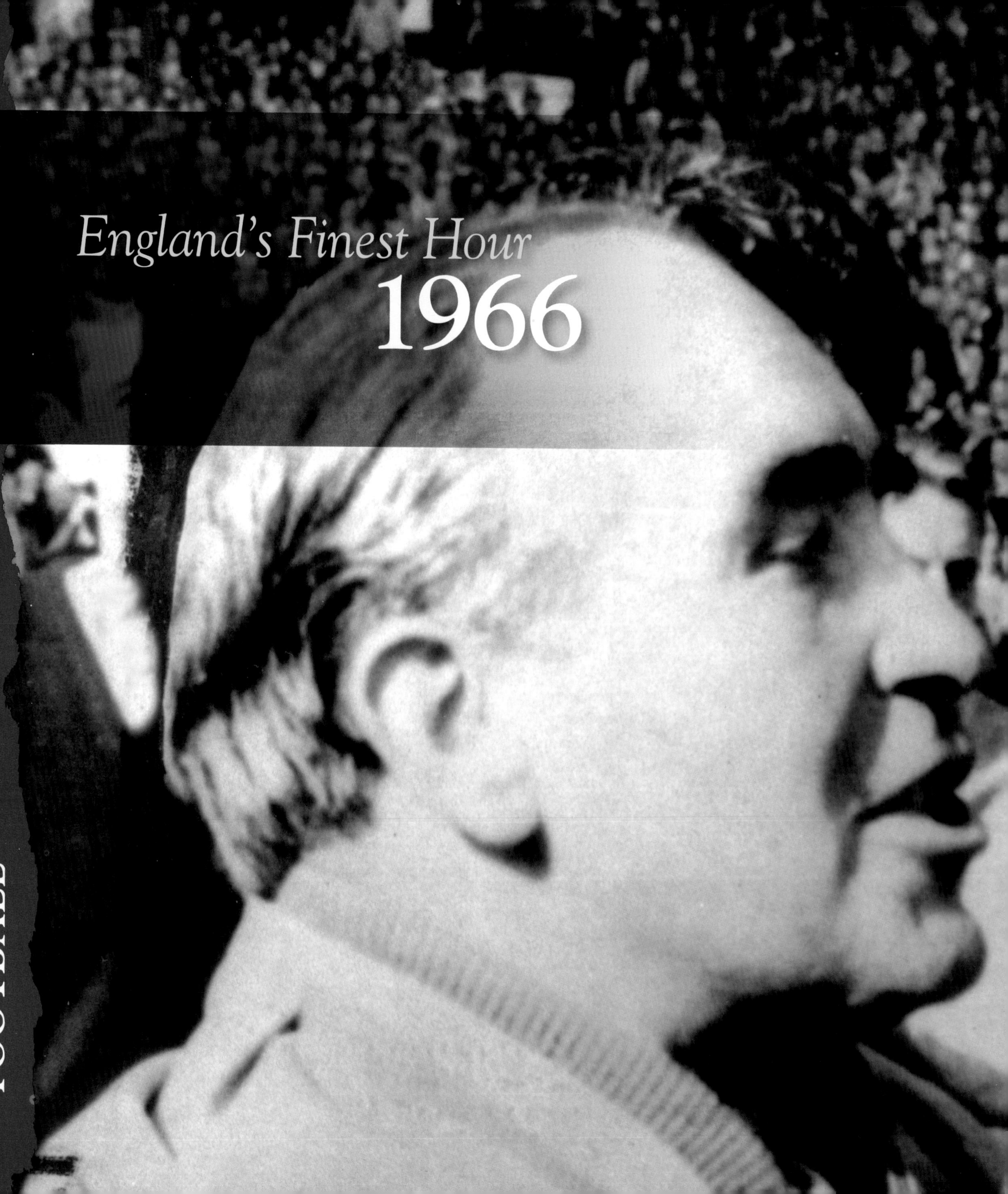

30th July 1966 and the greatest day in English football history. Manager Alf Ramsey, a professional to his core and one who rarely let his emotional guard down in public, savours an epic triumph with his skipper Bobby Moore. With the Jules Rimet trophy in their hands, England are the champions of the world.

In **1960** England was chosen as the host nation for the 1966 finals. The omens were good: they beat West Germany by 34 votes to 27 (without a luxury handbag for wives of FIFA officials in sight). In the lead-up to the tournament, **1963** was the year Alf Ramsey took over as England manager, due in large part to his title-winning exploits with Ipswich Town. He stated that England would win the World Cup in 1966. In **November 1965**, despite not being formally recognized by several western countries as a sovereign nation, North Korea defeated Australia in a playoff to decide who would be Asia's sole representative (the Aussies were grouped together with Asian sides). By **March 1966,** the football world was gearing up for what promised to be the best tournament yet – until calamity struck when the Jules Rimet trophy was stolen from an exhibition at the Central Hall in Westminster; thankfully it was found a week later by a dog called Pickles. On **11**th **July** the competition finally started but with something of a damp squib as England drew 0-0 with Uruguay. The tournament really kicked into life on **19**th **July** with North Korea's shock 1-0 win over Italy. By the time of the quarter-finals on **23**rd **July**, cup holders Brazil had been knocked out while England, West Germany and Portugal emerged as favourites to win the title. West Germany's 2-1 defeat of the Soviet Union on **25**th **July** and England's victory over Portugal a day later pitched the old adversaries against each other in the final on **30**th **July**.

LEFT: The *Daily Mirror*'s tournament staple: the World Cup wall chart, or in this case "scorecard".

The World Cup comes to colourful photographic life. For the first time the British media covered a tournament in appropriate detail, not least because it was played on home soil. Here in the renowned final against West Germany, goalkeeper Gordon Banks snuffs out a German attack.

England Welcomes the World

Sixteen teams from four continents journeyed to England for the tournament, held over three weeks in July.

Chile arrived at a rainy London Airport on 5th July. Note the bags plastered with the names of rival sports brands – an anomaly that modern exclusive sponsorship deals would no doubt prevent.

> *When at last the countries meet in the finals, the secrets become an open book.*
>
> Sir Alf Ramsey

RIGHT: Pelé was all smiles on arrival in England, acknowledged as the greatest player in the world, but he was to have a disappointing tournament.

The Soviet Union's legendary goalkeeper Lev Yashin readies himself for serious action and the impending Group 4 clash with North Korea at Middlesbrough's former ground, Ayresome Park.

"World Cup Willie", the first ever tournament mascot, takes it easy outside FA HQ in Lancaster Gate.

LEFT: A five-foot model of Willie took pride of place in 11-year-old Tina Neal's southeast London home after she won a Blue Peter competition. The model was made by Catherine Albers of East Sheen, whose mother said it was "too big for the house" and donated it to the programme as a prize. Here is Tina with *Blue Peter* presenter Valerie Singleton.

The Games Begin

The opening fixture was a disappointment, as England fought out a dull scoreless draw with Uruguay. Ramsey's 4-3-3 formation – dubbed the "wingless wonders" – could not break down the South Americans' rigid defensive rearguard.

LEFT: Poncho-wearing Mrs Reyna Garcia from Chile meets a rosette seller outside the stadium.

BELOW LEFT: Ken Bailey, England's self-appointed number-one fan who was a regular fixture at England games, welcomes a Mexican visitor beneath the Twin Towers.

BELOW: England skipper Bobby Moore introduces his team-mates to Her Majesty The Queen. They were to renew acquaintances three weeks later.

Luis Ubinas pursues Jimmy Greaves, England's much vaunted striker. Greaves came into the tournament as arguably the world's finest goalscorer, but his World Cup was soon to come to an end.

Goalkeeper Gordon Banks sums up England's frustration.

Despite their early exit, Brazil were glamorous and popular guests in England. Based in Lymm in Cheshire, they were the focus of huge attention from fans and media.

A lucky young autograph-hunter gets a lift courtesy of one of Brazil's coaching staff.

RIGHT: Goalkeeper Gilmar does a bit of shopping in Manchester.

Gerson carries Djalma Santos – yet it was Gerson who was suffering an injury.

St Michael
PIQUE NYLON
SHIRTS
DRIP-DRY PERFECTLY
SINGLE CUFFS
35/-

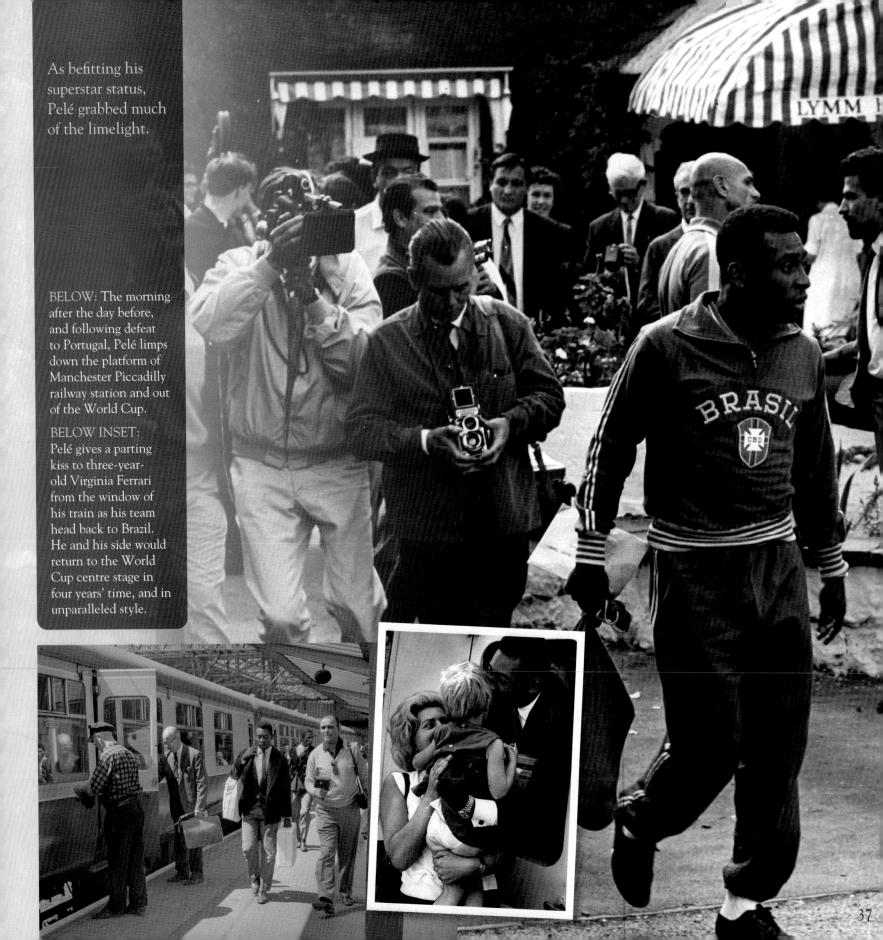

As befitting his superstar status, Pelé grabbed much of the limelight.

BELOW: The morning after the day before, and following defeat to Portugal, Pelé limps down the platform of Manchester Piccadilly railway station and out of the World Cup.

BELOW INSET: Pelé gives a parting kiss to three-year-old Virginia Ferrari from the window of his train as his team head back to Brazil. He and his side would return to the World Cup centre stage in four years' time, and in unparalleled style.

England had never seen anything like it: a host of exciting and exotic teams and players, plus thousands of visiting supporters drawn from around the world to witness what was the greatest football competition to date. The paying public responded with impressive enthusiasm, pushing the average attendance over the 50,000 mark for the first time in tournament history.

RIGHT: Linesman William Crawford carries off a collection of horns thrown onto the pitch before the Italy-Soviet Union game.

LEFT: Portugal's tough-tackling João Morais showed his tender side by rescuing a thrush from the Old Trafford pitch during the meeting with Bulgaria.

Not all the games were sell-outs: Only 15,000 saw the match between Chile and North Korea at Ayresome Park.

BELOW: The plight of referees officiating in crunch games has often been likened to stepping into the lions' den. Switzerland's Gottfried Dienst (left) and Germany's Rudolf Kreitlein paid an appropriate visit to Longleat and Lord Bath (centre) to meet a patriotic lion cub.

LEFT: Such was the passion generated by World Cup matches that media professionals could not suppress their national pride and loyalty. Here an over-enthusiastic Chilean photographer is removed from the pitch by policemen after his compatriot Ruben Marcos scored against the Soviet Union.

Sunderland's Roker Park was packed for the Group 4 tussle between the Soviet Union and Italy. The Soviets won 1-0.

England and West Germany's Road to Wembley

As the competition progressed, three teams emerged as front runners to lift the trophy: Portugal, inspired by the mercurial Eusebio; West Germany, an impressive blend of experience and youth personified by Uwe Seeler and 20-year-old Franz Beckenbauer; and the hosts – stripped of wingers and featuring few superstars, but bonded with an outstanding team ethic expertly assembled by Alf Ramsey.

With Bobby Charlton in athletic form, England made sure of qualification from Group 1 with a 2-0 win over a disappointing France, both goals were scored by Roger Hunt. The game was significant for another reason: Nobby Stiles' robust challenge on Jacques Simon prompted some members of the FA to tell Ramsey to drop the Manchester United midfielder. Ramsey refused: a point-blank rebuttal that broke decades of managerial subservience to bureaucratic grandees, and a sure sign of Ramsey's single-minded determination and modernist approach.

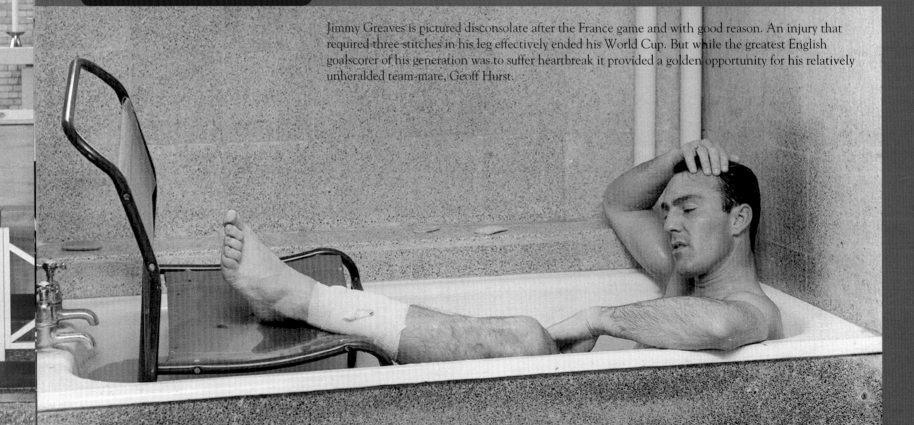

Jimmy Greaves is pictured disconsolate after the France game and with good reason. An injury that required three stitches in his leg effectively ended his World Cup. But while the greatest English goalscorer of his generation was to suffer heartbreak it provided a golden opportunity for his relatively unheralded team-mate, Geoff Hurst.

West Germany announced their presence with a 5-0 thumping of Switzerland in their first Group 2 match, featuring two goals from Beckenbauer (left) in front of a huge contingent of German fans packed on Hillsborough's Kop.

45

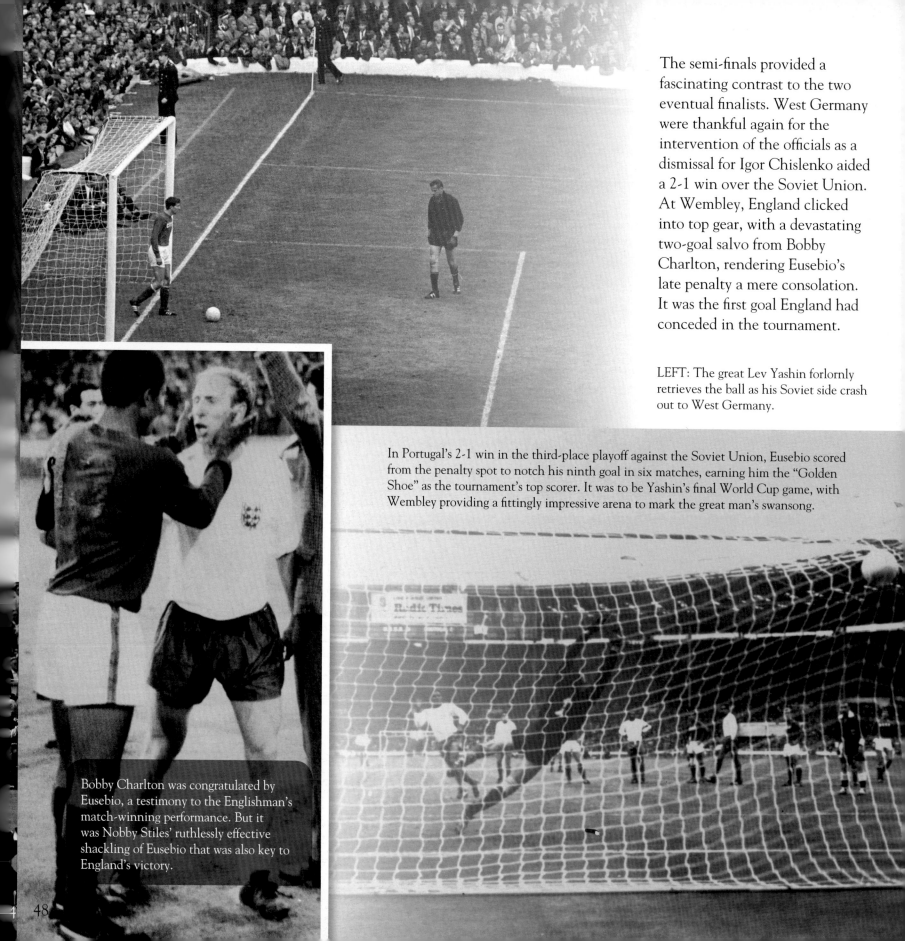

The semi-finals provided a fascinating contrast to the two eventual finalists. West Germany were thankful again for the intervention of the officials as a dismissal for Igor Chislenko aided a 2-1 win over the Soviet Union. At Wembley, England clicked into top gear, with a devastating two-goal salvo from Bobby Charlton, rendering Eusebio's late penalty a mere consolation. It was the first goal England had conceded in the tournament.

LEFT: The great Lev Yashin forlornly retrieves the ball as his Soviet side crash out to West Germany.

In Portugal's 2-1 win in the third-place playoff against the Soviet Union, Eusebio scored from the penalty spot to notch his ninth goal in six matches, earning him the "Golden Shoe" as the tournament's top scorer. It was to be Yashin's final World Cup game, with Wembley providing a fittingly impressive arena to mark the great man's swansong.

Bobby Charlton was congratulated by Eusebio, a testimony to the Englishman's match-winning performance. But it was Nobby Stiles' ruthlessly effective shackling of Eusebio that was also key to England's victory.

Bobby Charlton

–STAR–
OF THE TOURNAMENT

Mention the name of England's record goalscorer to a football fan – any football fan, anywhere in the world – and the reaction is likely to be a smile and respectful recognition for one of the game's genuine greats.

After a 20-year career for club and country, Charlton has come to symbolize all that is best about the British game: honest endeavour, dashing forward play and a passionate commitment to the sport. Having survived the Munich air disaster that devastated the famous Busby Babes, he became arguably the most famous player England has ever produced. In a team largely made up of effective but modest hard workers, Charlton offered a splash of ebullience and flair: the sight of the fleet-footed striker bursting through the middle, wispy hair trailing as he unleashed a venomous shot into the top corner of the net remains one of the game's most romantic and cherished images.

Football was in Charlton's blood. A nephew of the great Geordie folk hero Jackie Milburn, he was reputedly taught how to play from an early age by his mother Cissie. Here, the 15-year-old Bobby is tackled by Cissie and brothers Gordon and Tommy in 1953.

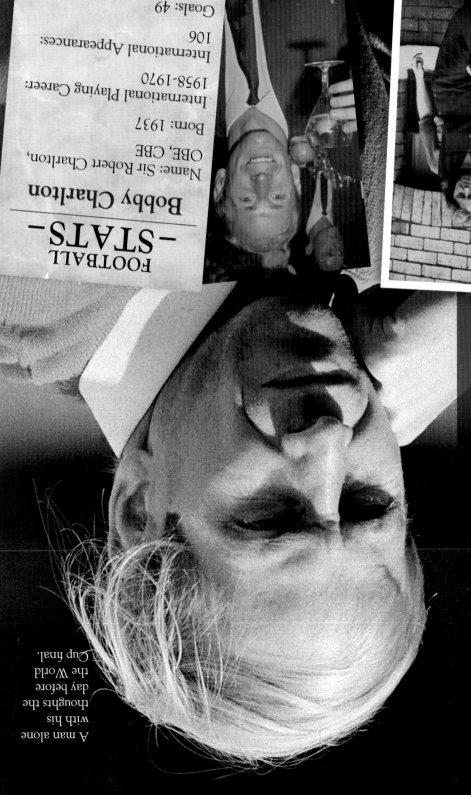

A man alone with his thoughts the day before the World Cup final.

–FOOTBALL–
–STATS–
Bobby Charlton

Name: Sir Robert Charlton, OBE, CBE

Born: 1937

International Playing Career: 1958-1970

International Appearances: 106

Goals: 49

BELOW: The focus of much of the players' attention was Ventura, due to appear alongside Cliff Richard in the film *Finders Keepers*. Jack Charlton kept an interest in what he had found, while Jimmy Greaves was similarly enamoured.

BELOW: Early on in the tournament the squad was treated to a visit to Pinewood film studios and share a drink or two with the stars. Sean Connery, shooting the 007 adventure *You Only Live Twice*, welcomed the players alongside Yul Brynner and glamorous starlet Vivienne Ventura. Connery and Bobby Moore (far right foreground) became firm friends – Connery once babysat for Moore's children, Dean and Roberta.

England Behind Closed Doors

With the eyes of a nation upon them and expectation reaching unprecedented levels, pressure mounted on the England players. Away from the games themselves, Ramsey and his management team strived to maintain the focus on the serious business of winning football matches, but there were lighter moments too, captured by the *Mirror's* photographers.

Left to right: Geoff Hurst, Nobby Stiles and Bobby Moore take things easy at Hendon Hall Hotel.

The squad did much of their preparation at the Bank of England sports ground at Roehampton. George Cohen (above) set the pace on the running track while there was a moment of laughter on the practice pitch (below).

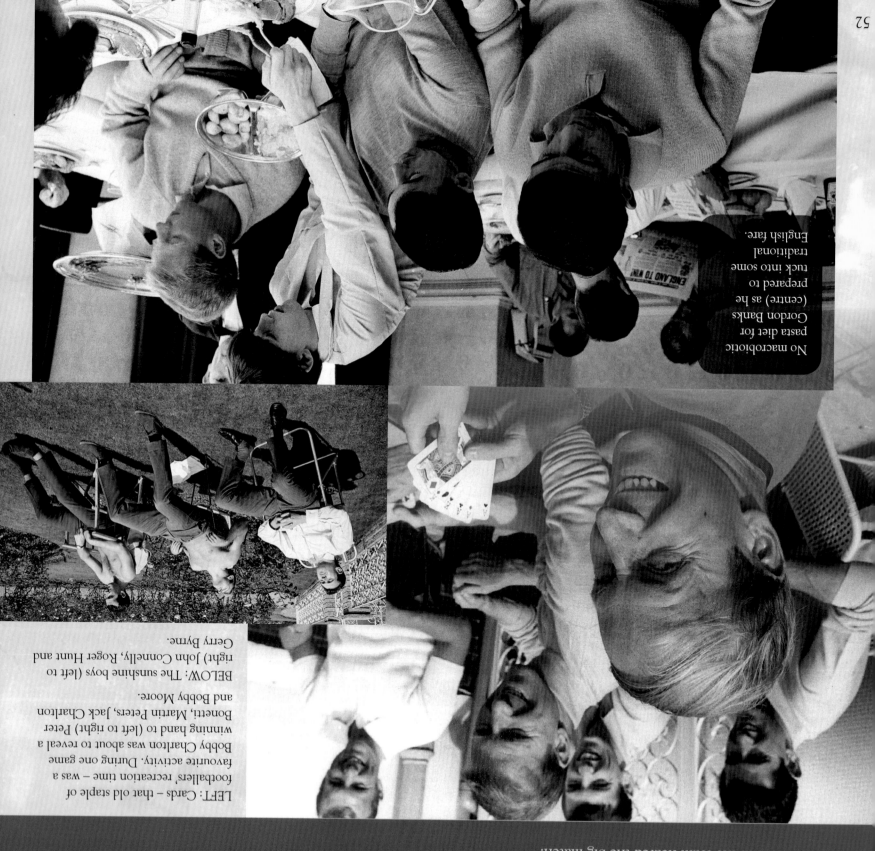

No macrobiotic pasta diet for Gordon Banks (centre) as he prepared to tuck into some traditional English fare.

LEFT: Cards – that old staple of footballers' recreation time – was a favourite activity. During one game Bobby Charlton was about to reveal a winning hand to (left to right) Peter Bonetti, Martin Peters, Jack Charlton and Bobby Moore.

BELOW: The sunshine boys (left to right) John Connelly, Roger Hunt and Gerry Byrne.

The squad were based at the Hendon Hall Hotel in northwest London – close to Wembley but quiet enough to avoid distractions as the team neared the big match.

ABOVE: Martin Peters may have been described by Ramsey as a player "10 years ahead of his time", but as the second youngest member of the squad the nerves began to show, as seen here on the team's departure from Hendon Hall for the trip to Wembley.

BELOW: Besieged by the media, Ramsey forced a smile as he evaluated his side's chances on the eve of the final.

Pursued by autograph-hunters, Bobby Moore was a picture of serious concentration.

As the day of the final drew near, tensions inevitably increased in the England camp.

30th July 1966, Wembley Stadium: there are 120 minutes on the clock; the scoreboard reads "England 3, West Germany 2" – and Geoff Hurst is about to write himself into sporting history and football legend.

England's Glory

Over 96,000 flocked to Wembley to witness the epic showdown between England and West Germany, while millions more tuned in on their TVs.

LEFT: Two hundred miles away in Paris, the monarch's uncle, the Duke of Windsor, settled down to watch the game.

BELOW AND BELOW INSET: Crowds mill around Wembley Way.

LEFT: Muhammad Ali, or Cassius Clay as he was then known, was one interested neutral. Clay was in the capital preparing for his August title fight against Brian London.

BELOW: Prime Minister Harold Wilson once claimed that England won the World Cup only when the Labour party was in power, but Tory leader Edward Heath was similarly not averse to basking in the reflected glory of the football team.

With Beckenbauer deputized to neutralize the threat of Bobby Charlton, the opening exchanges were tense and tight. West Germany drew first blood on 12 minutes after an error from Ray Wilson allowed Helmut Haller to rifle home; but six minutes later an unmarked Hurst headed home from Moore's quickly taken free-kick.

Nobby Stiles' industry was key to winning the midfield battle.

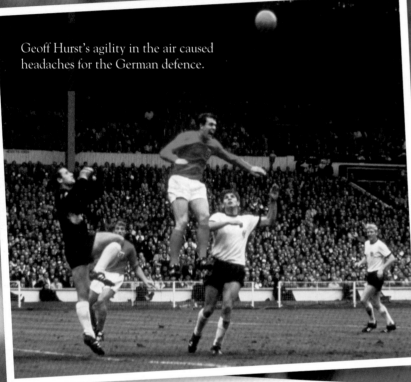

Geoff Hurst's agility in the air caused headaches for the German defence.

ENGLAND 1 GERMANY W. 1

ABOVE: For England's greatest football occasion, two young Irishmen on their summer holiday were given the considerable – and hazardous – responsibility of ensuring the scoreboard was accurately updated. Eighteen-year-old school pals Eddie O'Keeffe and Michael O'Sullivan had spent the summer in the UK and took on various jobs in order to fund the trip – one job resulted in their manning the scoreboard at Wembley.

Forty-three years later, Eddie found the pictures of himself and Michael on the *Daily Mirror's* football website and said: "It's fantastic. It brought back so many great memories. We were rooting for England – Bobby Charlton, Alan Ball and Bobby Moore were our heroes. We were right up in the roof and nothing was very secure. We would dread a goal because the whole place would start shaking – it was absolutely terrifying."

With chances at a premium in the second half, Martin Peters (No. 16) appeared to have given England the decisive breakthrough 12 minutes from time, pouncing on the loose ball with a powerful half-volley to make it 2-1...

...but West Germany's tenacious spirit was rewarded when Wolfgang Weber bundled the ball home with just a minute left to play. Bobby Moore appealed for handball to referee Gottfried Dienst but to no avail, with his crestfallen team-mates stunned at seeing victory snatched from them right at the death.

"

You've won it once – now go out and win it again.

Sir Alf Ramsey's comment to his players
before the start of extra time

"

With mentally and physically shattered players slumped on the Wembley turf, Ramsey called on all his motivational skills to reinvigorate his side.

The officials were also feeling the strain. Dienst took a well-earned rest, while linesman Karol Galba (left) and in particular Tofik Bakhramov (centre) readied themselves for what would be the most dramatic of contributions to subsequent events.

ABOVE: In the 11th minute of extra time came the game's pivotal incident and one of the most famous in all football. Latching on to a cross from the irrepressible Alan Ball, Hurst swivelled and crashed a shot onto the underside of the bar and over the line – or so the England players thought. Amid howls of protest from the Germans, Dienst consulted Bakhramov, and the Soviet linesman (or more accurately, Azerbaijani) ruled it was a valid goal.

Roger Hunt (centre) wheeled away to celebrate, certain that the ball had crossed the line. Controversy still rages today, with various computerized analyses suggesting the ball had or had not gone over the line; but hindsight cannot alter what happened on the day: England were 3-2 up.

It really was all over. With the final act of an unforgettable game, Hurst had scored his third (see pages 54–5) and, with the heads of Horst-Dieter Höttges (No. 2) and Wolfgang Overath bowed in despair, the West Ham striker exhaustedly embraced Alan Ball. Hurst had become the only player to date to score a hat-trick in a World Cup final, vindicating Ramsey's decision to drop Greaves and value work rate over individual flair. It was an oft-criticized strategy, but Ball in particular had epitomized the team's true qualities: supreme effort, a determined will to win and an unshakeable commitment to the team ethic.

It is one of the most famous images in British sporting history. Held aloft by his team-mates, Bobby Moore lifts the Jules Rimet to the ecstatic acclaim of a nation – and over 40 years on, it still has the power to move and inspire. The job of press photographers at the game, however, was not an easy one. They faced stringent restrictions for the 1966 final, with only a handful of officially sanctioned snappers allowed onto the touchline. The *Daily Mirror* had ace lensman Peter Cook providing an original insight on the game from the stands; meanwhile, his colleague John Varley had managed to find a way onto the pitch. Boy scouts were used as runners to convey messages between officials; Varley, deploying all his journalistic resourcefulness, donned a scout's armband and gained unique access to the action and the pitchside celebrations.

Ever the gentleman, Moore wiped his muddy hands on his shorts so as not to mark the Queen's white gloves as she presented the trophy.

Champions of the world, sealed with a kiss.

ABOVE: Amid the happy frenzy, a lone supporter paid homage at the goal net Hurst had virtually burst with his thunderous final shot.

The massed bands playing a celebratory refrain, as England embarked on a well-deserved lap of honour.

BELOW: And 40 years later the squad members who did not play in the final received their belated recognition with World Cup winner's medals presented by Gordon Brown at No. 10. FIFA had made a ruling to award replica medals for every player since 1930 who was part of a World Cup-winning squad.

Captain fantastic with his devoted team-mates.

> *There should be a law against him.*
> *He knows what's happening*
> *20 minutes before anyone else.*
>
> Jock Stein

FOOTBALL
—STATS—
Bobby Moore

Name: Robert Frederick
Moore OBE

Born: 1941

International Playing Career:
1962-1973

International Appearances:
108

Goals: 2

–STAR–
OF THE TOURNAMENT

Bobby Moore

Few players come to embody the spirit of the age they lived in; fewer still help define it. Bobby Moore is one such figure, a footballing legend who stands proud as an icon of the swinging Sixties.

The calm, unflappable heartbeat of Ramsey's team, Moore was arguably the most accomplished defender England has ever produced. Though he was not blessed with devastating pace, nor outstanding physical strengths, his unerring timing, comfort on the ball and exceptional ability to read a game made him the vital cog in Ramsey's well-oiled machine. It was his astute long-range pass that released Hurst for his third goal in the final – a perfectly measured assist when most other players would have aimed for row Z. On and off the pitch, Moore was the epitome of seemingly effortless cool: elegant, refined and unruffled, he was equally at home amid the intensity of a World Cup final or the glamour of a showbiz gathering – he was perhaps the only true modern superstar in the England side.

Moore was a larger than life character in many respects. Advertisers loved him: he could drink most of his peers under the table and was infamously (and falsely) accused of stealing jewellery just before the 1970 World Cup finals. He also bravely endured ill health, contracting testicular cancer in 1964, before bowel cancer cruelly ended his life in 1993 at the age of just 51. His death came far too soon, but if anything burnished the legend of the golden-haired hero whose image will never fade.

One of the sharpest of footballing dressers, Moore always looked the part.

The Country Rejoices

Wild celebrations began the moment the final whistle sounded. While the players enjoyed a sumptuous banquet, fans danced in the streets and the fun lasted well into the next day and beyond. Bobby Moore spent a quiet Sunday mowing the lawn back home; Jack Charlton woke up in a house in Leytonstone, and to this day is not quite sure how he got there.

RIGHT: Harold Wilson was swift to offer his acclaim at an official reception.

LEFT: The celebratory banquet for the players was held at the Royal Garden Hotel on Kensington High Street. Early arrivals included a group of German fans offering sporting, if slightly mystifying, congratulations.

69

Standing on the hotel balcony, Ramsey and his players took the plaudits from a huge crowd outside. Left to right: Terry Paine, George Cohen and Ramsey.

ABOVE: Hat-trick hero Geoff Hurst and his wife Judith arrived for the festivities, and Eusebio, the tournament's top scorer, offers his congratulations.

LEFT: Meanwhile, the players' wives, here reading about their husbands' exploits in the first editions of the *Sunday Mirror*, had to enjoy a separate dinner in the Royal Garden Hotel's Bulldog Lounge. The main reception was a strictly men-only affair and the couples only met up around midnight.

LEFT: Moore was the man in demand.

BELOW: Pickles, the dog that saved the World Cup, was an honoured party guest.

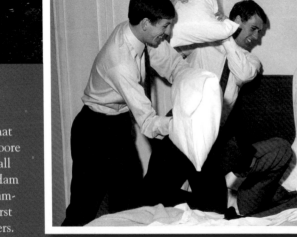

RIGHT: The morning after that night before, Moore got a wake-up call from his West Ham and England team-mates Geoff Hurst and Martin Peters.

Fans descended on Trafalgar Square to frolic in the fountains and proclaim victory from Nelson's column.

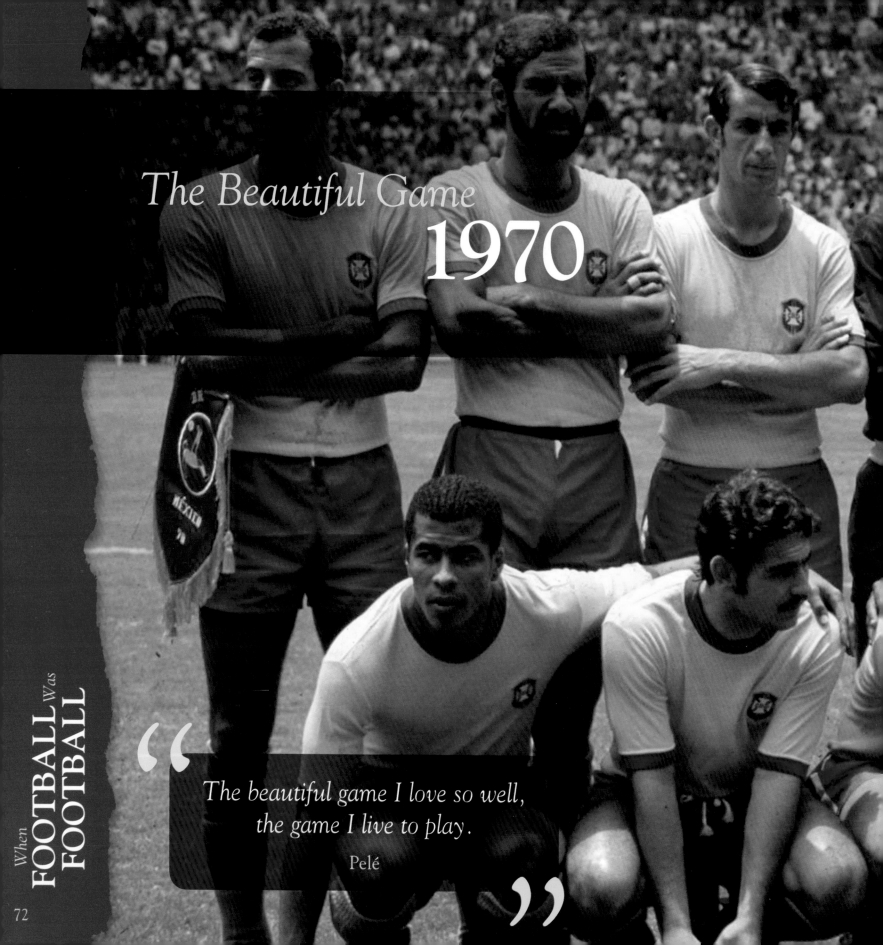

The Beautiful Game
1970

"
*The beautiful game I love so well,
the game I live to play.*

Pelé

"

The finest assembly of footballers ever to grace a pitch? Debate will always rage as to the best, but the clear candidate for many fans is the Brazil World Cup-winning line-up of 1970. Pictured before the group game against England are, left to right: (back row) Carlos Alberto (captain), Brito, Wilson Piazza, Felix, Clodoaldo, Everaldo; (front row) Jairzinho, Rivelino, Tostão, Pelé, Paulo Cesar. Cesar's place in the final was taken by Gerson, (inset).

Mexico was chosen as the host nation in 1964, the first country outside Europe or South America to have the honour. In 1969 João Saldanha resigned as manager of Brazil, protesting that his political affiliations had made him unpopular with the Brazilian establishment while also claiming Pelé was short-sighted and shouldn't be taken to the World Cup; Mario Zagallo took over. In July 1969, the infamous three-day "football war" broke out between El Salvador and Honduras; disputes around a World Cup qualifying match between the two nations sparked conflict that had been simmering for years over issues of immigration and economic tensions. By November 1969, Morocco had become the first African nation to qualify through a preliminary round for a World Cup final (Egypt had been invited in 1934). In May 1970, Bobby Moore was arrested and later released without charge after accusations that he had stolen a bracelet from a jewellers in Bogotá, Colombia, where reigning champions England were preparing for the finals. Four days into the tournament on 3rd June, Brazil gave notice of their intentions by thrashing Czechoslovakia 4-1 in their opening group game.

THE MATCHES

GROUP ONE Mexico City

May 31	Russia	Mexico
June 3	Belgium	El Salvador
June 6	Russia	Belgium
June 7	Mexico	El Salvador
June 10	Russia	El Salvador
June 11	Belgium	Mexico

Final Table	P	W	D	L	F	A	Pts
1							
2							
3							
4							

GROUP TWO Puebla-Toluca

June 2	Uruguay	Israel
June 3	Italy	Sweden
June 6	Uruguay	Italy
June 7	Israel	Sweden
June 10	Uruguay	Sweden
June 11	Israel	Italy

Final Table	P	W	D	L	F	A
1						
2						
3						
4						

QUARTER FINALS June 14

Winners Group One _____ v Second Group Two _____ (Mexico City)

Second Group One _____ v Winners Group Two _____ (Puebla-Toluca)

Winners Group Three _____ v Second Group Four _____ (Guadalajara)

Second Group Three _____ v Winners Group Four _____ (Leon)

SEMI FINALS

Winners 1st Quarter Final _____ v Winners 3rd Quarter Final _____ (Mexico City June 17)

Winners 2nd Quarter Final _____ v Winners 4th Quarter Final _____ (Guadalajara June 17)

FINAL June 21 (Mexico City)

Winners 1st Semi Final _____ Winners 2nd Semi Final _____

THE PLAYERS

THE 22 MEN WHO WILL DEFEND THE WORLD CUP

1 GORDON BANKS	2 KEITH NEWTON	3 TERRY COOPER	4 ALAN MULLERY	5 BR LA
Stoke City	Everton	Leeds Utd	Tottenham	Eve
Goalkeeper	Full-back	Full-back	Midfield	Def
Age: 32	Age: 28	Age: 25	Age: 28	Age
Caps: 59	Caps: 24	Caps: 8	Caps: 27	Cap

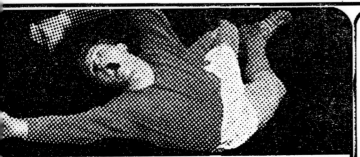

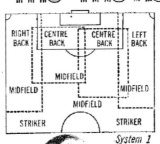
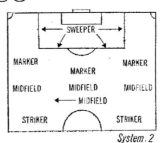
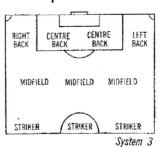

THE TACTICS And how Sir Alf will cope with them

System 1	System 2	System 3
RIGHT BACK / CENTRE BACK / CENTRE BACK / LEFT BACK — MIDFIELD — MIDFIELD MIDFIELD MIDFIELD — STRIKER STRIKER	SWEEPER — MARKER MARKER MARKER — MIDFIELD MIDFIELD MIDFIELD ← MIDFIELD — STRIKER STRIKER	RIGHT BACK / CENTRE BACK / CENTRE BACK / LEFT BACK — MIDFIELD MIDFIELD MIDFIELD — STRIKER STRIKER STRIKER

SYSTEM 1 This is the one Sir Alf Ramsey will adapt for England. The back four defenders mark loosely defined areas rather than individual attackers. Midfield players are expected to present the first line of defence and must work back behind the ball and offer challenge. They must be prepared to move quickly and intelligently in support of the strikers. The strikers will invariably be isolated. They need skill and courage to receive the ball under pressure until others can move forward in support. Expect Uruguay, Mexico, Rumania, Belgium, Sweden, Bulgaria and Israel to use this system as well as England.

SYSTEM 2 Caution is the keynote of this play — favoured by West Germany, Italy, El Salvador, Russia and other East European teams where they fear the individual skills of opponents. Defenders mark an individual, following him at all times. A player good at reading the game is used behind these defenders, providing them with cover. The free defender is known as the "sweeper." If an opponent has eluded his marker and advances on goal the "sweeper" must come out to offer challenge. Teams not prepared to work will suffer complete domination against this system.

SYSTEM 3 This is a variation of England's method. The difference is that there are three or four strikers and fewer players in midfield. Brazil will probably use it because of their confidence in the ability of outstanding attacking stars like Pele, Tostao, Jairzinho and Edu. The Brazilians are not as sound as their European opponents in defence and their great strength is in the improvisation of their individuals. The aim is to get the attackers into positions where opposing defenders cannot offer a collective challenge and where one burst can bring a goal. It is essential for the attack to retain its width.

GROUP THREE Guadalajara

2	Rumania	England
3	Czechoslovakia	Brazil
6	Rumania	Czechoslovakia
7	England	Brazil
10	Rumania	Brazil
11	England	Czechoslovakia

Table	P	W	D	L	F	A	Pts

GROUP OUR Leon

June 2	Peru	Bulgaria
June 3	Moro	W Germany
June 6	Peru	Morocco
June 7	Bulja	W Germany
June 10	Peru	W Germany
June 11	Bulja	Morocco

Final Table	P	W	D	L	F	A	Pts
1							
2							
3							
4							

THE CHAMPIONS

Winners-up _____

place: _____

place: _____

match to decide the 3rd and 4th positions takes place on June 20th at Iico City

Leon
Altitude 6,600 ft
Capacity 30,000

Guadalajara
Altitude 5,600 ft
Capacity 71,000

Mexico City
Altitude 7,500 ft
Capacity 109,000

Toluca
Altitude 8,800 ft
Capacity 29,000

Puebla
Altitude 7,100 ft
Capacity 35,000

miles
0   150   300

THE RECORD

Past World Cup Finals

1966	**England 4**	W. Germany 2
1962	**Brazil 3**	Czechoslovakia 1
1958	**Brazil 5**	Sweden 2
1954	**W. Germany 3**	Hungary 2
1950	**Uruguay**	(winners on a league basis)
1938	**Italy 4**	Hungary 2
1934	**Italy 2**	Czechoslovakia 1
1930	**Uruguay 4**	Argentina 2

BOBBY MOORE	7 FRANCIS LEE	8 ALAN BALL	9 BOBBY CHARLTON	10 GEOFF HURST	11 MARTIN PETERS	12 PETER BONETTI	13 ALEX STEPNEY	14 TOMMY WRIGHT	15 NOBBY STILES	16 EMLYN HUGHES	17 JACK CHARLTON	18 NORMAN HUNTER	19 COLIN BELL	20 PETER OSGOOD	21 ALLAN CLARKE	22 JEFF ASTLE
West Ham	Man City	Everton	Man Utd	West Ham	Tottenham	Chelsea	Man Utd	Everton	Man Utd	Liverpool	Leeds Utd	Leeds Utd	Man City	Chelsea	Leeds Utd	West Brom
Defender	Forward	Midfield	Midfield	Forward	Midfield	Goalkeeper	Goalkeeper	Full-back	Midfield	Full-back	Defender	Defender	Midfield	Forward	Forward	Forward
Age: 29	Age: 26	Age: 25	Age: 32	Age: 28	Age: 26	Age: 28	Age: 27	Age: 25	Age: 27	Age: 22	Age: 35	Age: 26	Age: 24	Age: 23	Age: 23	Age: 28
Caps: 80	Caps: 14	Caps: 41	Caps: 102	Caps: 38	Caps: 38	Caps: 6	Caps: 1	Caps: 9	Caps: 28	Caps: 6	Caps: 34	Caps: 13	Caps: 11	Caps: 1	Caps: 0	Caps: 3

Graphics by John Hill

75

LEFT: Jetting off to Mexico was 19-year-old secretary Michelle Tawil, who was wearing the official Brazil shirt made by her Cheshire employers Humphrey Bros. Ltd – later to be known as "Umbro".

LEFT: The opening game was a disappointment, with the hosts playing out a dull 0-0 draw with the Soviet Union. Yet the game was distinctive in another sense. For the first time, the World Cup was broadcast in colour on television. Red and yellow cards also made their debut, along with a system that allowed for two tactical substitutions per team.

A birds-eye view of the spectacular Azteca Stadium in Mexico City. Completed in 1966, it was the centrepiece of the tournament with space for 114,000 spectators and, even with a reduced current capacity of 105,000, is still one of the most impressive arenas in the world.

Anzor Kavazashvili, the Soviet goalkeeper, leaped to make a save.

BELOW: The commercial opportunities of the World Cup were also being realized to a greater degree. Adidas' Telstar football was the official ball, seen here in a publicity shot with models wearing shirts of (left to right) Mexico, England, Brazil and West Germany.

The Champions Prepare

England went into the tournament firmly among the favourites and with arguably a better squad than the one that had secured the trophy four years earlier. Physically the players were in top shape: in readiness for the debilitating heat of a Mexican summer they were subjected to rigorous medical tests before they left England.

The late Jeff Astle undergoes a blood test in December 1969.

Dental clinic
Reception

England's hat-trick hero Geoff Hurst waits his turn for a dental check at the Royal National Orthopaedic Hospital.

BACK HOME
World Cup Squad

Football songs have a long and mostly undistinguished history. One of the earliest and most successful examples was the England squad's 'Back Home', which got to Number One in April 1970. Here, Geoff Hurst hits the high notes.

England acclimatized to the soaring temperatures with a pre-tournament tour of Central and South America that ended in controversy.

ABOVE: Nobby Stiles "held up" Peter Osgood at the Rodeo in the old Olympic village in Mexico.

BELOW: Jack Charlton turned troubadour at a restaurant. But the relaxed mood gave no indication of the troubles the team, and Bobby Moore in particular, endured in Colombia.

Brian Kidd (left) and Allan Clarke compared tans with a female admirer as the team strolled around the Zona Rosa area of Mexico City.

Moore seen here with police investigators at the Green Fire shop in the Tequendama Hotel.

Bobby's Bogotá Nightmare

These remarkable pictures, never before published, reveal the extraordinary events behind one of England's most infamous World Cup episodes. On 18th May, while in Colombia preparing for the 1970 tournament, skipper Bobby Moore visited a hotel jeweller in Bogotá, along with Bobby Charlton to look at gifts for Charlton's wife. Accused by the sales assistant of stealing a bracelet worth £600, Moore was placed under house arrest for four days until pressure by the UK government led to Moore's release without charge.

In 2002, Foreign Office papers were opened which showed that the British Embassy had been informed that Colombian police knew the bracelet had in fact been stolen by a woman. One rumour is that a junior member of the squad stole the bracelet as part of a misguided prank. To this day, suspicion persists that the whole incident was a conspiracy to frame Moore and thus damage England's chances in the tournament.

Police interviewed Carla Padilla, the shop assistant who accused Moore.

Moore outside a Bogotá police station.

RIGHT: A bewildered
Moore leaves the
Tequendama Hotel
under escort.

81

Mexico's Football Fiesta

Pre-match celebrations at Cuauhtemoc for the Group 2 game between Uruguay and Italy. Mexico provided an exotic and stunning backdrop to what many football lovers still regard as the greatest World Cup tournament. Several teams – including England – relied on efficiency rather than expression in their tactical approach, but the tournament was studded with classic matches and memorable individual performances.

LEFT: Brazil's 4-1 Group 3 demolition of Czechoslovakia in Guadalajara was flattering: the Czechs scored first and had other chances, but the blistering goals of Pelé, Rivelino and a double from Jairzinho (left) provided ample evidence of the South Americans' all-round quality. The game is also famous for Pelé's attempted lob from the halfway line which beat Viktor but drifted just past the post.

ABOVE: Gerd Müller scored an impressive hat-trick in the 3-1 Group 4 defeat of Peru, and finished the tournament as top scorer with 10 goals, the best record since Just Fontaine's tally of 13 in 1958.

One of the great free-kick goals in the history of the World Cup: the Czech team looks on helplessly as Rivelino's wicked, rasping drive whistles through past the defensive wall and smacks into Viktor's goal.

The group tie everyone was waiting for came when Brazil took on the holders, England, in the suffocating heat of Guadalajara on 7th June. England were not popular among the locals. Ramsey had kept the Mexican media at arms length, noisy crowds gathered outside the team hotel to keep the players awake at night and the English were booed before kick-off.

ABOVE: Banks leaps to keep out a Brazilian effort. England held the golden hordes at bay for almost an hour thanks to two particularly brilliant passages of play. First, Banks somehow turned away Pelé's bullet header with what is commonly regarded as the greatest stop of all time. "At that time I hated Banks more than any man in football," Pelé said. "I just couldn't believe it. But when I cooled down I had to applaud him with all my heart. It was the greatest save I have ever seen." Then, in the second half, Moore stopped the galloping Jairzinho in his tracks with a perfectly timed and executed tackle.

Moore and Banks' heroics were to no avail, however. In the 59th minute, Tostão's trickery and strength enabled him to feed Pelé, who, with customary vision, laid the ball off for Jairzinho to power home.

> *Pelé was the most complete player I've ever seen.*
>
> Bobby Moore

> *He was my friend as well as the greatest defender I ever played against.*
>
> Pelé

RIGHT: The margin of victory for Brazil was a narrow one, but it put down a defining marker: Brazil were the team to beat. For two of the game's greatest players, however, there was nothing left to do but swap jerseys and pay mutual respect.

West Germany's Revenge

ABOVE: England got off to a great start when Alan Mullery's adroit near-post finish gave them the lead after 31 minutes. Martin Peters added a second four minutes after the break and England appeared to be home and dry. However, Franz Beckenbauer pulled one back on 68 minutes, slipping a shot under Bonetti's body.

ABOVE: In what was to prove a key factor in the outcome of the quarter-final meeting in Leon with West Germany, Peter Bonetti took the place of Gordon Banks in goal for England. Banks had succumbed to a stomach bug – rumours circulated that it was more than just an accidental upset – and while Bonetti was an outstanding and experienced keeper, his nervous display contributed to England's demise. Seeler's rather fortunate, looping back header in the 76th minute brought the teams level, and for the second World Cup in a row extra time beckoned for the two sides.

In his record-setting 106th appearance for his country, a dejected Bobby Charlton left the field in the 70th minute consoled by Alf Ramsey and in so doing bade farewell to international football. Ramsey was criticized by some for Charlton's withdrawal and that of Martin Peters 11 minutes later, but West Germany's dogged never-say-die attitude was probably more fundamental to the outcome. Müller scored from close range in the 18th minute of extra time to seal a remarkable comeback.

–STAR–
OF THE TOURNAMENT

Pelé

The origins of the nickname are still something of a mystery, but the moniker Pelé is famous around the globe as that of the finest player the world has ever seen. He emerged from childhood poverty to become a national hero in Brazil and an icon for any fan of the sport. But his fame transcended mere popular appeal; when he played an exhibition match in Nigeria in 1969, the two sides in the Biafran war downed weapons for a 48-hour ceasefire so that combatants could watch the maestro in action.

Pelé had it all: speed, strength, skill, flawless technique and a lethal shot despatched from either foot. He was a fine dribbler, passer and reader of play, and brilliant in the air. There were simply no weaknesses in his game. Though he could be physically stopped, as illustrated by the dreadful treatment he was exposed to by defenders in 1966, he could also tough it out with the most uncompromising opponents. He played to high standards of sportsmanship, but was not afraid to give as good as he got.

By 1970, at the age of 29, he was at his peak. The Brazil side perfectly complemented his qualities, with the craft and guile of Gerson, Tostão and Rivelino, the pace of Jairzinho and the leadership of Carlos Alberto combining to help enable Pelé to perform to his sublime, mesmerizing, magical best.

> *Pelé is the greatest player of all time. He reigned supreme for 20 years. All the others – Diego Maradona, Johann Cruyff, Michel Platini – rank beneath him. There's no one to compare with Pelé.*
>
> Franz Beckenbauer

> *I think instead of calling the game football, we should call it Pelé.*
>
> Romario

The perfect blend of power and poise.

ABOVE: Pelé eludes Alan Mullery in the midst of what was a terrific contest between the two. The England midfielder recalled of their duel: "I hugged him after the final whistle. 'You are the cleanest player I have ever played against,' he told me. I didn't know what to say. It was a wonderful accolade from a brilliant player."

Pelé is universally popular wherever he goes, as on this trip to Wembley in 1987.

FOOTBALL –STATS–

Pelé

Name: Edson Arantes do Nascimento – "Pelé"

Born: 1940

International Playing Career: 1957-1971

International Appearances: 92

Goals: 77

The Final Four

After quarter-final wins for Italy (hitting form with a 4-1 victory against the hosts), Uruguay (beating the Soviet Union 1-0), and Brazil's 4-2 triumph against Peru, the semi-final line-up was complete.

Brazil took on their South American neighbours Uruguay in Guadalajara. Now firmly established as favourites with bookmakers and neutrals, the Brazilians limbered up at their hotel on the eve of the contest.

BELOW: Uruguay were difficult opponents. They took the lead through Luis Cubilla, and their robust approach threatened to upset the Brazilians' rhythm, including Pelé (left) and Jairzinho, (right).

Eventually, Brazil's class told, with goals from the eye-catching Clodoaldo, Jairzinho and Rivelino. Pelé was absent from the scoresheet, but almost scored the goal of the century at the death. Tostão brilliantly played him in and, as goalkeeper Ladislao Mazurkiewicz ran out to challenge, Pelé executed an outrageous dummy, collected the ball and nearly squeezed in a low shot from an acute angle.

LEFT: In the other semi-final, Italy survived a trademark West German comeback to win 4-3 after extra time, a result that went down well with the locals inside the Azteca.

The Golden Boys

En route to the final against Italy, Brazilian players were mobbed.

Edu (left) and Pelé (right) tried to get some sleep on the plane from Guadalajara to Mexico City.

ABOVE: A winner as a player in 1958 and 1962, manager Mario Zagallo, known as "The Professor", employed a tactical approach that did not initially go down well with the 1970 generation. However, he allowed his multi-talented charges free rein to express themselves during the finals with spectacular results, employing a fluid formation that allowed the full-backs to venture deep into the opposition half, complementing the flair of a star-studded midfield and attack. Zagallo was a Brazilian World Cup winner yet again in 1994, as Carlos Alberto Parreira's technical director.

The final presented a fascinating clash of styles, with Brazil's faith in expansive, often unstoppable flair against Italy's resolute defence. Despite the potent attacking threat of Gigi Riva, Sandro Mazzola and Roberto Boninsegna, the Italians tended towards the *catenaccio* ethos of safety first, and were determined to snuff out Brazil's fluency at source. It was to prove a vain task.

91

O Rei

The king of football punches the air as he celebrates scoring in the 1970 World Cup. Pelé gave Brazil the lead in the final with a prodigious leap and bullet header, emphatically beating Enrico Albertosi in the Italian goal. Fittingly, it was Brazil's 100th goal in the competition.

> "I told myself before the game, 'he's made of skin and bones just like everyone else'. But I was wrong."
>
> Tarcisio Burgnich, Italian defender

93

After Italy had equalized through Boninsegna, Brazil regained the lead in the 66th minute, courtesy of Gerson's viciously struck low shot. Jairzinho's seventh goal of the tournament five minutes later made the result safe, before the final goal four minutes from time. This encapsulated what made Brazil so special: Clodoaldo shimmied and swerved past four Italian midfielders and passed to Rivelino. He played an incisive pass down the left flank to Jairzinho who instantly brought the ball under control, before pivoting to cut inside and feed Pelé. With uncanny awareness, instead of taking a shot himself Pelé played a simple ball out to the right for the barnstorming Carlos Alberto to crack home. "That was sheer, delightful football," said Kenneth Wolstenholme in the BBC commentary box. Never was a truer word said about the beautiful game.

Brazil's victory was arguably the most popular in the history of the World Cup, such was the worldwide admiration for their class and style. As Carlos Alberto lifted the Jules Rimet trophy, presented in perpetuity to Brazil in honour of their third triumph, ecstatic supporters spilled onto the pitch in a frenzy of celebration, mobbing their heroes and even tearing off their kit.

Total Fußball
1974

Three of the 1974 World Cup's pivotal figures, captured together in action. West Germany goalkeeper Sepp Maier writhes in apparent agony after a challenge by Netherlands' Johann Cruyff (left), while Franz Beckenbauer appeals for a foul.

In 1971 FIFA commissioned a replacement for the Jules Rimet trophy with the chosen design created by Silvio Gazzaniga. It was cast in gold, weighed 11 pounds and was 20 inches high. West Germany's victory in the 1972 European Championships installed them as favourites to win the World Cup two years later. In October 1973 a 1-1 draw at Wembley with Poland meant England failed to qualify for the finals; Scotland finished top of Group 8 and booked their place in a World Cup finals for the first time since 1958. In November 1973, the Soviet Union's political objections to travel to Chile for the return leg of their qualifying playoff meant the South Americans were rewarded with a walkover. With a record 97 sides entering the competition, the range of competing teams broadened, with Australia, Zaire and Haiti representing new names added to the list of World Cup finals participants. Also in 1973, Ajax completed their hat-trick of European Cup wins adhering to the "Total Football" philosophy devised by former manager Rinus Michels, installed as coach of the Dutch national side in 1974. On 17th May 1974, Bayern Munich won the European Cup with six players who would go on to play in the World Cup for their national team. João Havelange took over as FIFA President from Sir Stanley Rous after the Ordinary Congress in Frankfurt on 11th June. The tournament began on 13th June with a change of format: a second stage comprising two groups of four and then the final replaced the more familiar knockout arrangement of quarter-finals following a single qualifying stage.

DAILY MIRROR

WHAT'S ON TV DAY BY DAY

THURSDAY, JUNE 13
OPENING CEREMONY, 5.0 p.m.
Live B.B.C.-1, I.T.V, Reports Radio 2
BRAZIL v. YUGOSLAVIA, Frankfurt, 5.0 p.m.
OTHER PROGRAMMES: B.B.C, Highlights, 10.15 p.m.

FRIDAY, JUNE 14
SCOTLAND v. ZAIRE, Dortmund, 7.30.
E. GERMANY v. AUSTRALIA, Hamburg, 7.30.
B.B.C Highlights, Reports Radio 2
W. GERMANY v. CHILE, W. Berlin, 7.30.
Live B.B.C.-1, Reports Radio 2
OTHER PROGRAMMES: B.B.C, Highlights, 10.45 p.m.
I.T.V, Highlights, 12.25 a.m.

SATURDAY, JUNE 15
URUGUAY v. HOLLAND, Hanover, 4.0.
POLAND v. ARGENTINA, Stuttgart, 6.0.
Live B.B.C.-1, Reports Radio 2
SWEDEN v. BULGARIA, Dusseldorf, 4.0.
ITALY v. HAITI, Munich, 6.0.
Live I.T.V, Reports Radio 2
OTHER PROGRAMMES: B.B.C, Match of the Day, 1.20 p.m.

SUNDAY, JUNE 16
B.B.C, Match of the Week, 1.55 p.m. I.T.V, Round-up, 2.0 p.m.

MONDAY, JUNE 17
B.B.C, World Cup Report, 6.55 p.m. I.T.V, Holland v. Uruguay (recording), 10.25 a.m. World Cup Scene, 5.20 p.m.

TUESDAY, JUNE 18
SCOTLAND v. BRAZIL, Frankfurt, 7:30.
Live B.B.C.-1, I.T.V, Radio 2
AUSTRALIA v. W. GERMANY, Hamburg, 4.0.
Live B.B.C.-1, Reports Radio 2
YUGOSLAVIA v. ZAIRE, Gelsenkirchen, 7.30.
Reports Radio 2
CHILE v. E. GERMANY, W. Berlin, 7.30.
Reports Radio 2
OTHER PROGRAMMES: B.B.C, Highlights, 10.55 p.m. I.T.V., World Cup Scene, 5.20; Highlights, 11.0 p.m.

WEDNESDAY, JUNE 19
ARGENTINA v. ITALY, Stuttgart, 7.30.
Live I.T.V, Reports Radio 2
HOLLAND v. SWEDEN, Dortmund, 7.30.
BULGARIA v. URUGUAY, Hanover, 7.30.
HAITI v. POLAND, Munich, 7.30.
B.B.C.-1, Action from Dortmund, Honover and Munich, Reports Radio 2
OTHER PROGRAMMES: B.B.C, Highlights 10.25 p.m. I.T.V Morning Match (recording), 10.25 a.m.; World Cup Scene, 5.20; Highlights, 11.0 p.m.

THURSDAY, JUNE 20
B.B.C, World Cup Report, 6.50 p.m. I.T.V, Morning Match (recording), 10.25 a.m.; World Cup Scene, 5.20 p.m.

FRIDAY, JUNE 21
B.B.C, World Cup Report, 6.45 p.m. I.T.V, Morning Match (recording), 10.25 a.m.; World Cup Scene, 5.20 p.m.

SATURDAY, JUNE 22
SCOTLAND v. YUGOSLAVIA, Frankfurt, 4.0.
Live B.B.C.-1, I.T.V, Radio 2
E. GERMANY v. W. GERMANY, Hamburg, 7.30.
Live B.B.C.-1, I.T.V, Radio 2
ZAIRE v. BRAZIL, Gelsenkirchen, 4.0.
Reports Radio 2
AUSTRALIA v. CHILE, W. Berlin, 4.0.
Reports Radio 2

SUNDAY, JUNE 23
POLAND v. ITALY, Stuttgart, 4.0.
Live I.T.V, Reports Radio 2
BULGARIA v. HOLLAND, Dortmund, 4.0.
SWEDEN v. URUGUAY, Dusseldorf, 4.0.
ARGENTINA v. HAITI, Munich, 4.0.
B.B.C.-1, Action from Dortmund, Dusseldorf and Munich
OTHER PROGRAMMES: B.B.C, To be announced.
I.T.V, Highlights and Round-up of First Round, 3.0 p.m.; Highlights, 11.15 p.m.

MONDAY, JUNE 24
B.B.C, To be announced. I.T.V, Morning Highlights, 11.0 a.m., World Cup Scene, 5.20 p.m.

TUESDAY, JUNE 25
B.B.C, To be announced. I.T.V, Morning Match (recording), 10.25 a.m.; World Cup Scene, 5.20 p.m.

WEDNESDAY, JUNE 26
FOUR SECOND SERIES GAMES
B.B.C, and I.T.V live coverage to be announced.
OTHER PROGRAMMES: B.B.C, To be announced.
I.T.V, Highlights, 11.0 p.m.

THURSDAY, JUNE 27 AND FRIDAY, JUNE 28
B.B.C, To be announced. I.T.V, Morning Match (recording), 10.25 a.m.; World Cup Scene, 5.20 p.m.

SATURDAY, JUNE 29
B.B.C, Grandstand. I.T.V, World of Sport.

SUNDAY, JUNE 30
FOUR SECOND SERIES GAMES
Live coverage by B.B.C and I.T.V to be announced.
I.T.V, Highlights, 11.15 p.m.

MONDAY, JULY 1 AND TUESDAY, JULY 2
B.B.C, To be announced. I.T.V, Morning Match (recording), 10.25 a.m.; World Cup Scene, 5.20 p.m.

WEDNESDAY, JULY 3
FOUR SECOND SERIES GAMES
Live coverage by B.B.C and I.T.V to be announced.
I.T.V, Highlights, 11.0 p.m.

THURSDAY, JULY 4
B.B.C, To be announced. I.T.V, Highlights, 11.0 p.m. World Cup Scene, 5.20 p.m.

FRIDAY, JULY 5
B.B.C, To be announced. I.T.V, Morning Match (recording), 10.25 a.m.; World Cup Scene, 5.20 p.m. Who'll win the Cup?, 10.30 p.m.

SATURDAY, JULY 6
THIRD PLACE PLAY-OFF, Munich, 4.0.
Live B.B.C.-1, I.T.V, Reports Radio

SUNDAY, JULY 7
THE FINAL, Munich, 4.0. Live B.B.C.-1, I.T.V, Radio

THE SCOTLAND WORLD CUP SQUAD

1 DAVID HARVEY	2 SANDY JARDINE	3 DANNY McGRAIN	4 BILLY BREMNER	5
Leeds	Rangers	Celtic	Leeds	
Goalkeeper	Defender	Defender	Midfield	
Age: 26	Age: 24	Age: 23	Age: 31	
Caps: 7	Caps: 16	Caps: 12	Caps: 47	

A grim-faced Sir Alf Ramsey confronted the reality of England's surprise qualification failure, after Poland's 1-1 draw at Wembley. Poland's performance was inspired by the goalkeeping heroics of Jan Tomaszewski, dubbed a "clown" before the game by Brian Clough.

JUST two days to go before Brazil kick off the 1974 World Cup against Yugoslavia in Frankfurt . . . and make history.

It's the first time the competition hasn't been launched by the host nation. West Germany surrendered that honour to commemorate Brazil's hat-trick of World Cup triumphs (1958, 1962 and 1970), which won them the Jules Rimet Cup outright. But here in Britain, all eyes will be on Billy Bremner and his Scottish squad as they set out hopefully on the road to the Final in Munich on July 7.

The Scots—in the same group as Brazil and Yugoslavia—launch their World Cup attack against Zaire in Dortmund . . . which can be seen live on both B B C and I T V.

During the next three weeks the sixteen nations will play thirty-eight matches in nine West German centres to decide who is the first holder of the new eighteen carat gold F I F A World Cup (right) valued at £17,000, but priceless to the winning team.

RON WILLS

1930—URUGUAY 4	ARGENTINA 2
1934—ITALY 2*	CZECHOSLOVAKIA 1
1938—ITALY 4	HUNGARY 2
1950—URUGUAY 2	BRAZIL 1
1954—W. GERMANY 3	HUNGARY 2
1958—BRAZIL 5	SWEDEN 2
1962—BRAZIL 3	CZECHOSLOVAKIA 1
1966—ENGLAND 4*	W. GERMANY 2
1970—BRAZIL 4	ITALY 1
	*After extra time

YOUR SCORE CHART

AFTER the First Series of games, decided on a league basis (two points for a win, one for a draw), the top two teams in Groups 1, 2, 3 and 4 form Groups A and B in the Second Series. Group A is formed by the winners of Groups 1 and 3 and the runners-up in Groups 2 and 4; Group B by the winners of Groups 2 and 4 and the runners-up in Groups 1 and 3. Each qualifying team is given a key letter and number to indicate its fixtures in the Second Series. Thus, if Scotland win Group 2, they become B6. If they are runners-up they will be A2. The eventual winners of Groups A and B meet in the Final. The runners-up meet in the third-place play-off.

GROUP ONE

June 14	W. Germany	Chile
June 14	E. Germany	Australia
June 18	Chile	E. Germany
June 18	Australia	W. Germany
June 22	Australia	Chile
June 22	E. Germany	W. Germany

Final Table
	P	W	D	L	F	A	Pts
A1							
B5							

GROUP TWO

June 13	Brazil	Yugoslavia
June 14	Zaire	Scotland
June 18	Yugoslavia	Zaire
June 18	Scotland	Brazil
June 22	Zaire	Brazil
June 22	Scotland	Yugoslavia

Final Table
	P	W	D	L	F	A	Pts
B6							
A2							

GROUP THREE

June 15	Sweden	Bulgaria
June 15	Uruguay	Holland
June 19	Holland	Sweden
June 19	Bulgaria	Uruguay
June 23	Bulgaria	Holland
June 23	Sweden	Uruguay

Final Table
	P	W	D	L	F	A	Pts
A3							
B7							

GROUP FOUR

June 15	Italy	Haiti
June 15	Poland	Argentina
June 19	Haiti	Poland
June 19	Argentina	Italy
June 23	Argentina	Haiti
June 23	Poland	Italy

Final Table
	P	W	D	L	F	A	Pts
B8							
A4							

GROUP A

June 26	A1	A4
June 26	A2	A1
June 30	A1	A3
June 30	A4	A2
July 3	A4	A1
July 3	A3	A2

SECOND SERIES

GROUP A
	P	W	D	L	F	A	Pts
1							
2							
3							
4							

GROUP B
	P	W	D	L	F	A	Pts
1							
2							
3							
4							

GROUP B

June 26	B6	B5
June 26	B7	B8
June 30	B5	B7
June 30	B8	B6
July 3	B8	B5
July 3	B7	B6

THIRD PLACE PLAY-OFF

July 6, Olympic Stadium, Munich

RESULT _____

WORLD CUP FINAL

July 7, Olympic Stadium, Munich

RESULT _____

JOHN ... 7 JIMMY JOHNSTONE Celtic Forward Age: 29 Caps: 22 | 8 KEN DALGLISH Celtic Midfield Age: 23 Caps: 19 | 9 JOE JORDAN Leeds Forward Age: 22 Caps: 11 | 10 DAVID HAY Celtic Midfield Age: 26 Caps: 24 | 11 PETER LORIMER Leeds Forward Age: 25 Caps: 13 | 12 THOMSON ALLAN Dundee Goalkeeper Age: 26 Caps: 2 | 13 JIM STEWART Kilmarnock Goalkeeper Age: 20 Caps: 0 | 14 MARTIN BUCHAN Man Utd Defender Age: 25 Caps: 13 | 15 PETER CORMACK Liverpool Midfield Age: 27 Caps: 8 | 16 WILLIE DONACHIE Man City Defender Age: 24 Caps: 11 | 17 DONALD FORD Hearts Forward Age: 29 Caps: 3 | 18 TOMMY HUTCHISON Coventry Forward Age: 27 Caps: 7 | 19 DENIS LAW Man City Forward Age: 35 Caps: 54 | 20 WILLIE MORGAN Man Utd Midfield Age: 28 Caps: 18 | 21 GORDON McQUEEN Leeds Defender Age: 21 Caps: 1 | 22 ERIC SCHAEDLER Hibs Defender Age: 24 Caps: 1

Scotland, by contrast, could look forward to the tournament with high hopes after a successful qualification campaign led by skipper Billy Bremner.

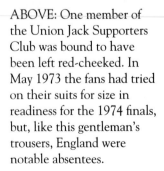

ABOVE: One member of the Union Jack Supporters Club was bound to have been left red-cheeked. In May 1973 the fans had tried on their suits for size in readiness for the 1974 finals, but, like this gentleman's trousers, England were notable absentees.

Scots Miss

As the sole representative of the British Isles, Scotland went into the tournament under manager Willie Ormond as the focus of much media attention. Boasting a good squad with both experience and quality, they could not make it past a tough group stage, but were the only unbeaten side at the tournament.

RIGHT: Getting into sartorial shape, the Scotland squad were kitted out in official C&A suits (£29.99 each at the time) and took along mascot Rory Superscot.

BELOW: Into the studio to record their World Cup song 'Scotland Scotland' were (left to right) manager Willie Ormond, George Connelly, Erich Schaedler, Jim Holton, Donald Ford, songwriter Bill Martin, Willie Morgan, Denis Law, Sandy Jardine, and Danny McGrain, with Kenny Dalglish and Tom Forsyth at the back.

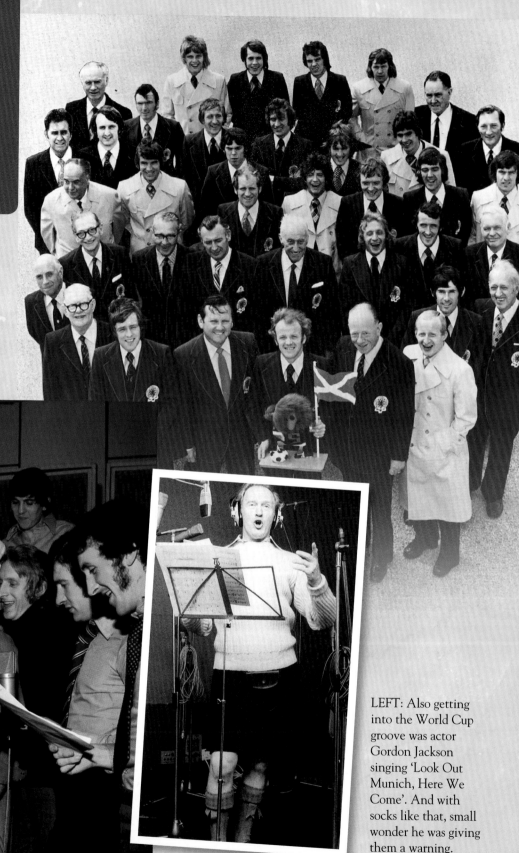

LEFT: Also getting into the World Cup groove was actor Gordon Jackson singing 'Look Out Munich, Here We Come'. And with socks like that, small wonder he was giving them a warning.

Conditions were better suited for European sides than their counterparts from sunnier parts of the world. The rain that dampened the opening ceremony became a feature of the tournament.

ABOVE: Wrapping up for the evening kick-off, Brazil fans brought their usual dash of colour for the game against Scotland.

LEFT: Scotland got off to a good start with a 2-0 win over newcomers Zaire, with Denis Law in acrobatic action.

Joe Jordan gets in a header in the 0-0 Group 2 draw with Brazil. Though the holders were a shadow of their brilliant 1970s selves, missing the likes of Pelé, Tostão and Gerson, the result was still an admirable one for the Scots. With another draw against tough opposition in the shape of Yugoslavia, Scotland finished the group tied with Brazil and Yugoslavia on four points, and only exited the competition on goal difference.

Billy Bremner walks off the pitch dejected at the end of the Yugoslavia match. Yugoslavia had been in sharpshooting form in their 9-0 win over Zaire.

New Faces, New Looks

Haiti gave a respectable account of themselves in their 3-1 defeat to Italy. Here, Giacinto Facchetti swaps pennants with Wilner Nazaire.

ABOVE: East Germany versus Australia was an eye-catching new fixture. The Germans won 2-0, with goalkeeper Jürgen Croy fending off John Warren.

LEFT: Zaire were popular newcomers, not least when Mwepu Ilunga broke from the defensive wall in the game against Brazil and hoofed the ball away, before Brazil had taken the free kick. The Leopards left without scoring a goal and conceded 14, but as sub-Saharan Africa's first World Cup competitors, they opened up a path that many other sides from the region have since followed.

In the decade that fashion forgot, footballers great and lesser-known made their distinctive mark.

Brazil's Rivelino sported a more hirsute look.

The great Johnny Rep went for an off-the-shoulder style.

Lock up your daughters – it's Argentina's Ruben Ayala.

Haiti's Henry Francillon cut a slightly more elegant figure.

As the competition hotted up, two teams emerged as clear favourites. With South America's representatives on the wane, it was left to European neighbours West Germany and the Netherlands to contest the final.

> *Simple football is the most beautiful. But playing simple football is the hardest thing.*
>
> Johann Cruyff

The Dutch "total football" system was based on a revolutionary principle: every player in the team could effectively play in any position. When a defender moved forward into attack, for example, a midfielder could cover his position. This retained the team's organizational structure but enabled a fluidity of passing and movement that was gloriously effective and a joy to watch. A direct counter to the defensive *catenaccio* system, it relied on having outstanding players who could put it into practice. Opponents were left bewildered – none more so than Sweden's full-back Jan Olsson, who was bamboozled by Cruyff's famous turn in their Group 3 meeting. Team-mate Inge Ejderstedt (above) was given a similar run-around by Cruyff and his team-mates Ruud Krol, Johan Neeskens, and Johnny Rep.

ABOVE: Total Football was rarely bettered than in the 4-0 destruction of Argentina. The two sides met in the Group A second round phase, and the Dutch cut through the Argentines at will, with Cruyff evading Daniel Carnevali to score the first goal.

RIGHT: Argentina barely got a sniff of a chance, and in frustration Roberto Perfumo found his way into referee Bob Davidson's book.

The hosts fielded an impressive mix of collective experience and individual talent, well organized by manager Helmut Schön. Yet they got off to a mediocre start, not helped by contractual disputes behind the scenes. Australia and Chile were brushed aside easily enough, but the lukewarm reception from the home fans indicated all was not initially well.

LEFT: The shock of the first group stage came when East Germany defeated their western counterparts 1-0. A match loaded with Cold War tensions, the fixture was not a one-off – there had been five prior meetings between the divided countries in Olympic qualifiers – but Jürgen Sparwasser's winner was a headline grabber beyond the football pitch. Ironically, the defeat did West Germany a favour: by finishing second in their group, they avoided the Netherlands in the next phase.

West Germany improved as the tournament progressed. They beat Yugoslavia 2-0 thanks to goals from Paul Breitner and Gerd Müller (left). Sweden were then vanquished 4-2, with Wolfgang Overath (right) getting on the scoresheet before the decisive Group B meeting with Poland.

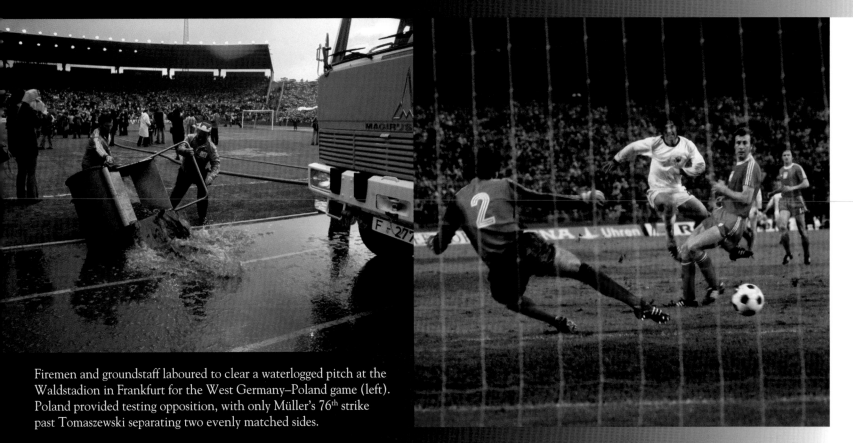

Firemen and groundstaff laboured to clear a waterlogged pitch at the Waldstadion in Frankfurt for the West Germany–Poland game (left). Poland provided testing opposition, with only Müller's 76th strike past Tomaszewski separating two evenly matched sides.

With the second group phase decided, West Germany and the Netherlands met in the final. It pitted two football philosophies against each other – Dutch Total Football versus German precision and teamwork, exemplified in two giants of the era.

–STAR–
OF THE TOURNAMENT

Franz Beckenbauer

In over 30 years as player and manager, Franz Beckenbauer won medals galore to provide glittering evidence of his awesome talent. Yet his standing in the sport rises beyond titles and trophies. "Der Kaiser" shaped how the game itself is played, helping to define the role of the sweeper, or *libero*, and making the position his own. A prodigiously gifted young player, he burst on to the international stage in the 1966 World Cup, gilded his reputation four years later and hit his peak on home soil in 1974. With the West Germans under intense pressure and scrutiny, Beckenbauer was the resolute and determined heart of the team, a dominating presence in pulling strings from his vantage point just behind the defence and springing into attack when the opportunity arose.

A three-time European Cup winner with Bayern Munich, Beckenbauer joined Pelé to take part in the great American soccer experiment with New York Cosmos, before embarking on a managerial career that culminated with masterminding the national side's third World Cup victory in 1990, thus becoming the first man to win the trophy both as captain and coach.

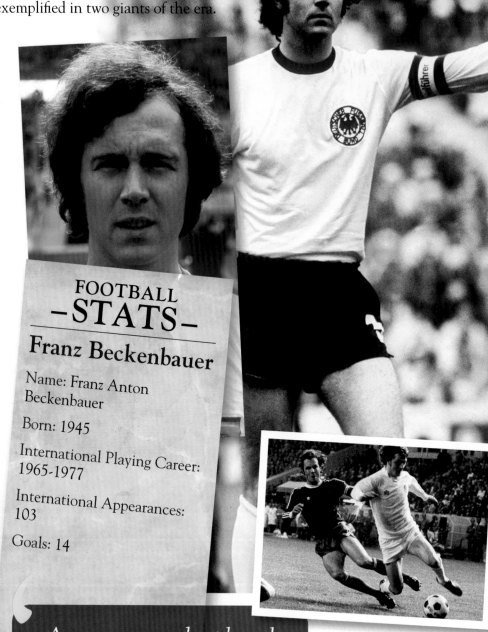

FOOTBALL
–STATS–

Franz Beckenbauer

Name: Franz Anton Beckenbauer

Born: 1945

International Playing Career: 1965-1977

International Appearances: 103

Goals: 14

"
As someone who played a team sport, I feel a bit uncomfortable being ranked as an individual so high.

Franz Beckenbauer
"

ABOVE: Beckenbauer was just as dominant at club level, competing here for Bayern Munich against Leeds in the 1975 European Cup final.

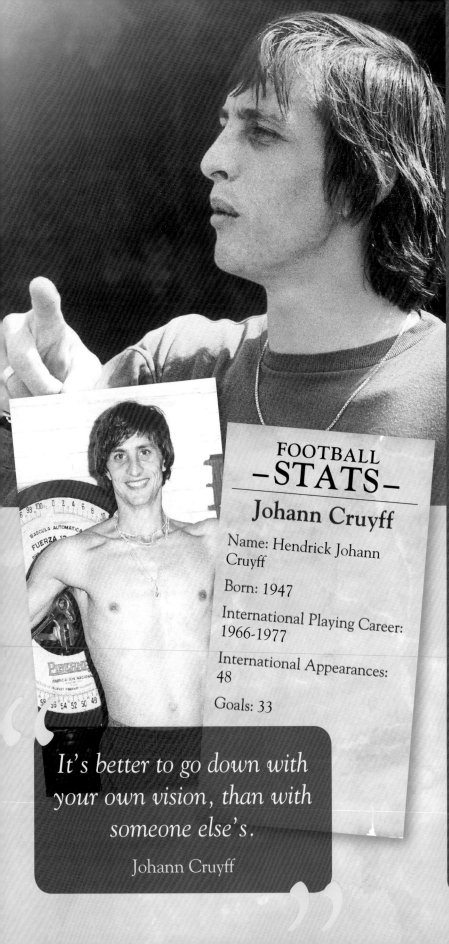

–STAR–
OF THE TOURNAMENT

Johann Cruyff

Widely regarded as the finest European player of all time, Cruyff was the total footballer. Able to switch effortlessly from a central striking role to the flank, or come deep and confuse his opponents, Cruyff dictated games like few others have ever been able to. With a range of bewilderingly effective passing, a whip crack turn of pace, a feint, shimmy or trademark "Cruyff" turn, the Dutchman could unlock even the tightest defence. As a goalscorer there have been few better, illustrated by a strike rate of almost 1.5 goals per game at international level. His Dutch career was relatively brief with just 48 appearances in the famous orange shirt and only the one World Cup finals appearance. Missing the 1978 tournament apparently in objection to the Argentinean regime, it later transpired that a kidnap threat against his family had influenced his decision to retire early from international football.

Brought up in the Ajax Total Football academy with whom he won three European Cup medals, Cruyff was a cigarette-smoking free spirit whose character embodied the liberal Dutch stereotype. He became a legend at Barcelona, readily identifying with Catalonian culture, but has often faced accusations of being too opinionated – a feature of Dutch players that has inspired but also perhaps worked against their so-far frustrated attempts to win football's ultimate prize.

RIGHT: In mesmerizing action against Argentina. Note that Cruyff has only two black stripes on his shirt, as opposed to the three of kit suppliers Adidas that his team-mates wore. Cruyff had his own deal with arch rivals Puma and insisted on just the two stripes.

FOOTBALL
–STATS–

Johann Cruyff

Name: Hendrick Johann Cruyff

Born: 1947

International Playing Career: 1966-1977

International Appearances: 48

Goals: 33

It's better to go down with your own vision, than with someone else's.

Johann Cruyff

Munich's Olympiastadion provided a futuristic arena for what was a very modern closing ceremony and World Cup final – a spectacle televised around the word, and a game in which tactical systems won the day.

The game started in astonishing fashion. The Netherlands kicked off, and in an object lesson of Total Football principles, scored without the Germans even touching the ball. Barely a minute of precise control and movement from the Dutch ended with Uli Hoeness tripping Cruyff. Referee Jack Taylor gave a penalty and Neeskens rifled home.

ABOVE: The Dutch failed to press home the advantage. Driven on by the remorseless Beckenbauer, West Germany worked tirelessly to close Cruyff and his compatriots down.

Hoeness takes the game to the Dutch.

After Paul Breitner had equalized from the spot, West Germany scored the winning goal two minutes before the break thanks to the marksmanship of Gerd Müller. The 1970 Golden Boot winner seized on a cross from Rainer Bonhof and swivelled to fend off the attentions of Ruud Krol (12) and Arie Haan.

The Dutch came back strongly in the second half, but thanks in large part to a gutsy display from Sepp Maier, the Germans were able to stand firm and see out the win.

"The Kaiser" victorious.

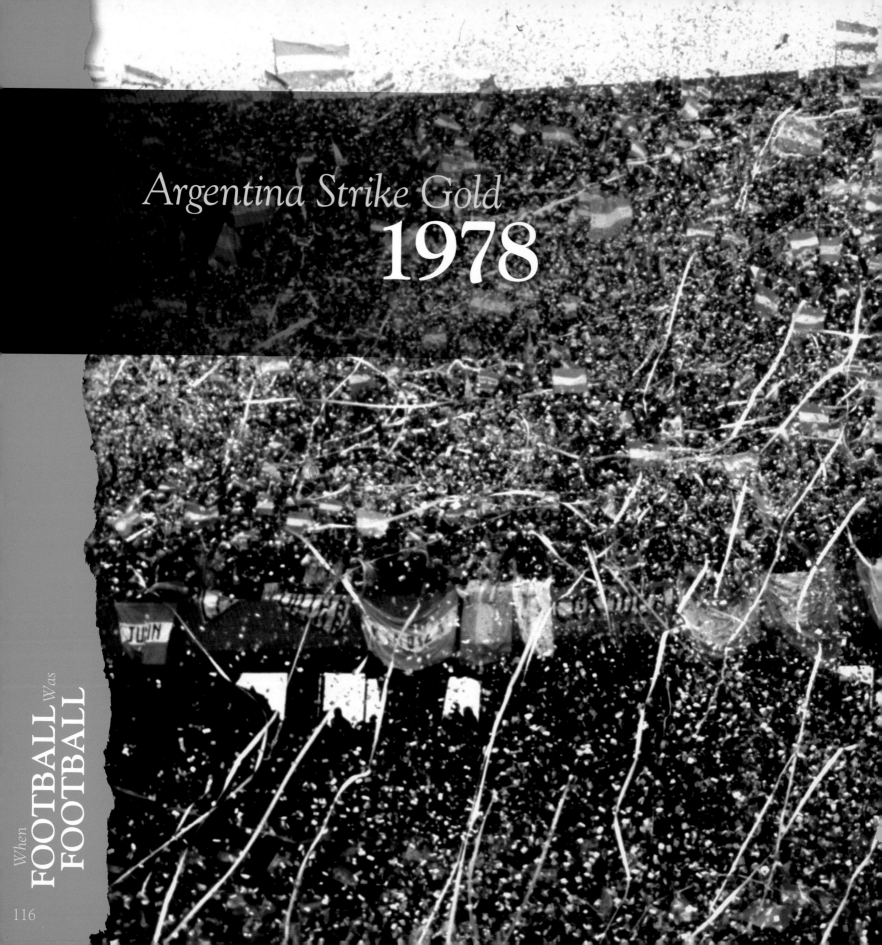

Argentina Strike Gold
1978

Colour, noise and the passion of a people desperate for success in troubled times – Argentina provided a series of unforgettable World Cup memories, notably the incredible atmosphere that greeted the hosts onto the field of play.

VILLA MAZA

In **1974**, following a disappointing tournament in West Germany, the Argentinean FA appointed César Luis Menotti as coach of the national side. Two years later, in **1976,** Argentina's government was deposed in a military coup led by General Jorge Videla. It was rumoured that several countries, including the Netherlands, considered a World Cup boycott in protest. In the end all 16 nations took part, though German defender Paul Breitner stayed at home. England's 2-0 defeat to Italy in Rome on **17**[th] **November** ultimately meant the 1966 winners failed to qualify for the second tournament in succession. Scotland's controversial victory over Wales in **October 1977** booked their place in the finals. Iran joined the World Cup club after ending a marathon qualifying campaign in **December 1977**. As World Cup year swung round in **1978**, Coca Cola were announced as the competition's first official sponsor. Penalty shoot-outs were allowed for knockout games level after extra time, but not required as both the third place playoff and final were settled within 120 minutes. **2**[nd] **June 1978** saw the World Cup debut of a certain French midfielder called Michel Platini. Argentina began their attempt to win the World Cup for the first time on the same day, but without the 17-year-old Diego Maradona, whom Menotti had left out of the squad. Scotland's Willie Johnston was banned after a failed drugs test following the shock defeat to Peru on **3**[rd] **June**. Rob Rensenbrink's penalty for the Netherlands against Scotland on **11**[th] **June** was the 1,000[th] goal in the World Cup.

DAILY MIR

GOOD LUCK TO ALLY AND HIS ARMY

SCOTLAND'S World Cup bid kicks off against Peru in faraway Argentina on Saturday. Ally MacLeod's men are representing all of us. Wherever you come from in Britain—Land's End or John O'Groats—you will be wishing them well.

There have been doubts about staging the tournament in Argentina, concern about Scotland's recent form. That is history now. The World Cup, a feast of football, is almost under way and the Scots are there with the best wishes of every British fan.

1 ALAN ROUGH	2 SANDY JARDINE	3 WILLIE DONACHIE	4 MARTIN BUCHAN	5 GORDON McQUEEN	6 BRUCE RIOCH	7 DON MASSON	8 K
Partick Keeper Age: 26 Caps: 17	Rangers Defender Age: 29 Caps: 32	Man C Defender Age: 26 Caps: 30	Man U Defender Age: 29 Caps: 26	Man U Defender Age: 25 Caps: 19	Derby Mid-field Age: 30 Caps: 21	Derby Mid-field Age: 31 Caps: 15	

12 JIM BLYTH	13 STUART KENNEDY	14 TOM FORSYTH	15 ARCHIE GEMMILL	16 LOU MACARI	17 DEREK JOHNSTONE	18 GRAEME SOUNESS	19
Coventry Keeper Age: 23 Caps: 2	Aberdeen Defender Age: 25 Caps: 3	Rangers Defender Age: 29 Caps: 18	Nottm F Mid-field Age: 31 Caps: 24	Man U Mid-field Age: 28 Caps: 23	Rangers Forward Age: 24 Caps: 11	Liverpool Mid-field Age: 25 Caps: 5	

YOUR DAY BY DAY TV

THURSDAY, 1 JUNE
OPENING CEREMONY: 5.45 p.m.
Live: BBC-1 ITV, Radio 2 Reports.

WEST GERMANY v POLAND: Buenos Aires,
7.00 p.m.
Live: BBC-1 (6.50 p.m.), ITV, Radio 2 (6.33 p.m.).

FRIDAY, 2 JUNE
FRANCE v ITALY: Mar del Plata, 5.45 p.m.
Live: ITV (5.30 p.m.) Highlights: BBC-1 (10.15 p.m.).
HUNGARY v ARGENTINA: Buenos Aires,
11.15 p.m.
Live: BBC-1 (11.05 p.m.)

TUNISIA v MEXICO: Rosario, 8.45 p.m.
Highlights: BBC-1 (10.15 p.m.)
OTHER PROGRAMMES: ITV: W. Germany v Poland repeat
(10.25 a.m.), Radio 2: 6.33 p.m, World Cup report (11.02 p.m.).

SATURDAY, 3 JUNE
PERU v SCOTLAND: Cordoba 8.45 p.m.
Live: BBC-1 (8.20 p.m.), ITV, Radio 2 (8.30 p.m.).
SWEDEN v BRAZIL: Mar del Plata, 5.45 p.m.
Live: BBC-1 (5.25 p.m.), Highlights: ITV (8.15 p.m.).
SPAIN v AUSTRIA: Buenos Aires, 5.45 p.m.
Live: ITV (5.15 p.m.). Highlights: BBC-1.
IRAN v HOLLAND: Mendoza, 8.45 p.m.
Highlights: B.B.C.1 (10.30 p.m.)
OTHER PROGRAMMES: ITV: World Cup '78 (12.35 p.m.)
Radio 2: Report (01.15 a.m.). Report (8.30 p.m.) Sports
Desk (11.02 p.m.)

SUNDAY, 4 JUNE
ITV: Highlights of Sweden v Brazil and Iran v Holland
(2.15 p.m.).

MONDAY, 5 JUNE
B.B.C.-1: Report 6.50 p.m. Radio 2: 6.33 p.m.

TUESDAY, 6 JUNE
MEXICO v WEST GERMANY: Cordoba, 8.45 p.m.
Live: BBC-1 (8.35 p.m.).
ITALY v HUNGARY: Mar del Plata, 5.45 p.m.
Live: ITV (5.30 p.m.). Highlights: BBC-1.
ARGENTINA v FRANCE: Buenos Aires, 11.15 p.m.
Live: BBC-1 (11.05 p.m.).
POLAND v TUNISIA: Rosario, 8.45 p.m.
Live: ITV (8.40 p.m.). Highlights: BBC-1
OTHER PROGRAMMES: Radio 2: Report (6.33 p.m. and
11.02 p.m.).

WEDNESDAY, 7 JUNE
SCOTLAND v IRAN: Cordoba, 8.45 p.m.
Live: BBC-1 (8.30 p.m.), ITV, Radio 2 (8.30 p.m.).
BRAZIL v SPAIN: Mar del Plata, 5.45 p.m.
Live: BBC-1 (5.30 p.m.). Highlights: ITV (8.15 p.m.).
AUSTRIA v SWEDEN: Buenos Aires, 5.45 p.m.
Live: ITV (5.30 p.m.). Highlights: BBC-1.
HOLLAND v PERU: Mendoza, 8.45 p.m.
Highlights: BBC-1 (10.30 p.m.)
OTHER PROGRAMMES: ITV: World Cup '78 plus Derby
(1.00 p.m.) Radio 2: Report (01.15 a.m.). Sports Desk
(6.33 p.m.). Report (8.30 p.m.).

THURSDAY, 8 JUNE
BBC-1: Report 7.00 p.m.). ITV: World Cup '78 Highlights
etc. (1.00 p.m. and 5.15 p.m.). Radio 2: Sports Desk
(6.33 p.m.).

FRIDAY, 9 JUNE
BBC-1: Report (6.50 p.m.). Radio 2: Sports Desk (6.33 p.m.).

SATURDAY, 10 JUNE
ITALY v ARGENTINA: Buenos Aires, 11.15 p.m.
Live: ITV, Radio 2.
FRANCE v HUNGARY: Buenos Aires, 5.45 p.m.
Live: BBC-1 (5.30 p.m.). Highlights: ITV (8.30 p.m.).
MEXICO v POLAND: Rosario, 8.45 p.m.
Live: ITV. Highlights: BBC-1 (10.35 p.m.).
TUNISIA v W. GERMANY: Cordoba, 8.45 p.m.
Live: BBC-1 (8.25 p.m.). Highlights: ITV (10.45 p.m.).
OTHER PROGRAMMES: ITV: World Cup '78 (12.35 p.m.).

SUNDAY, 11 JUNE
SCOTLAND v HOLLAND: Mendoza, 8.45 p.m.
Live: BBC-1 (8.15 p.m.). ITV, Radio 2 (8.30 p.m.).
PERU v IRAN: Cordoba, 8.45 p.m.
Highlights: BBC-1 (10.30 p.m.).
SWEDEN v SPAIN: Buenos Aires, 5.45 p.m.
Live: ITV (5.30 p.m.). Highlights: BBC-1.
BRAZIL v AUSTRIA: Mar del Plata, 5.45 p.m.
Live: BBC-1 (5.30 p.m.). Highlights: ITV (8.15 p.m.).
OTHER PROGRAMMES: BBC-1: Highlights Italy v Argentina
(11.15 a.m.). ITV: France v Hungary, Tunisia v W. Germany
Highlights 2.15 p.m. Radio 2: Sports Desk (11.02 p.m.).

MONDAY 12 JUNE
BBC-1: Report (6.45 p.m.). ITV: World Cup '78 (1.00 p.m.).
World Cup Special (5.15 p.m. Radio 2: Sports Desk (6.33 p.m.).

TUESDAY 13 JUNE
BBC-1: Report (6.45 p.m.). Radio 2: Sports Desk (6.33 p.m.).

18

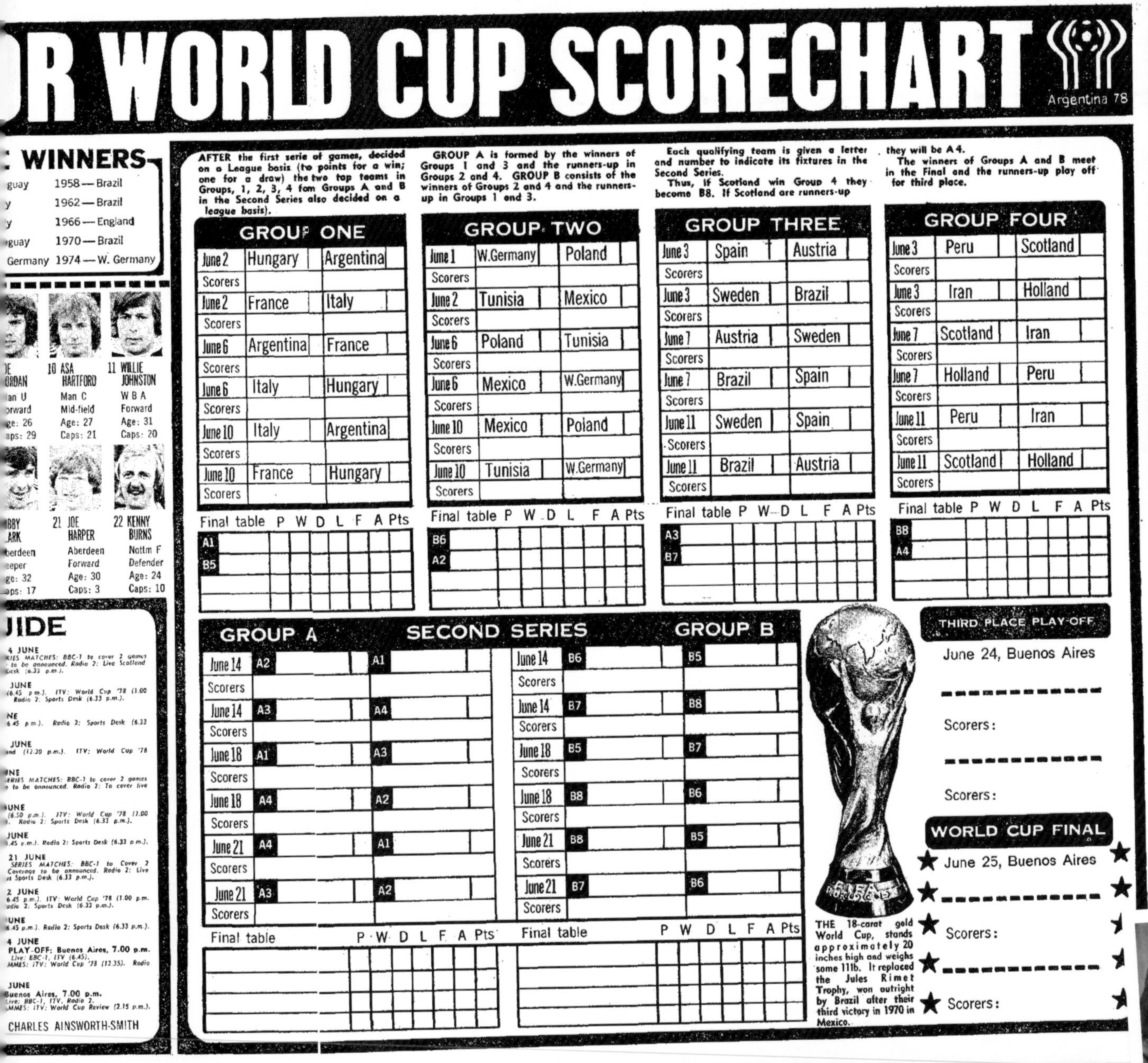

…R WORLD CUP SCORECHART

Argentina 78

…WINNERS

…guay 1958 — Brazil
…y 1962 — Brazil
…y 1966 — England
…guay 1970 — Brazil
Germany 1974 — W. Germany

…E …ORDAN
…an U
…orward
…ge: 26
…aps: 29

10 ASA HARTFORD
Man C
Mid-field
Age: 27
Caps: 21

11 WILLIE JOHNSTON
W B A
Forward
Age: 31
Caps: 20

…BBY …ARK
…berdeen
…eeper
…ge: 32
…aps: 17

21 JOE HARPER
Aberdeen
Forward
Age: 30
Caps: 3

22 KENNY BURNS
Nottm F
Defender
Age: 24
Caps: 10

…IDE

4 JUNE
…RIES MATCHES: BBC-1 to cover 2 games … to be announced. Radio 2: Live Scotland …Desk (6.33 p.m.).

JUNE
(6.45 p.m.). ITV: World Cup '78 (1.00 … Radio 2: Sports Desk (6.33 p.m.).

…NE
6.45 p.m.). Radio 2: Sports Desk (6.33

JUNE
…nd (12.30 p.m.). ITV: World Cup '78

…NE
…ERIES MATCHES: BBC-1 to cover 2 games … to be announced. Radio 2: To cover live

…UNE
(6.50 p.m.). ITV: World Cup '78 (1.00 … Radio 2: Sports Desk (6.33 p.m.).

JUNE
…45 p.m.). Radio 2: Sports Desk (6.33 p.m.).

21 JUNE
SERIES MATCHES: BBC-1 to Cover 2 Coverage to be announced. Radio 2: Live …s Sports Desk (6.33 p.m.).

2 JUNE
6.45 p.m.). ITV: World Cup '78 (1.00 p.m. …adio 2: Sports Desk (6.33 p.m.).

…UNE
6.45 p.m.). Radio 2: Sports Desk (6.33 p.m.).

4 JUNE
PLAY-OFF: Buenos Aires, 7.00 p.m.
Live: BBC-1, ITV (6.45).
…MMES: ITV: World Cup '78 (12.35). Radio

JUNE
Buenos Aires, 7.00 p.m.
Live: BBC-1, ITV, Radio 2.
…MMES: ITV: World Cup Review (2.15 p.m.).

CHARLES AINSWORTH-SMITH

AFTER the first serie of games, decided on a League basis (to points for a win; one for a draw) the two top teams in Groups, 1, 2, 3, 4 fom Groups A and B in the Second Series also decided on a league basis).

GROUP A is formed by the winners of Groups 1 and 3 and the runners-up in Groups 2 and 4. GROUP B consists of the winners of Groups 2 and 4 and the runners-up in Groups 1 and 3.

Each qualifying team is given a letter and number to indicate its fixtures in the Second Series.

Thus, if Scotland win Group 4 they become B8. If Scotland are runners-up they will be A4.

The winners of Groups A and B meet in the Final and the runners-up play off for third place.

GROUP ONE

June 2	Hungary	Argentina
Scorers		
June 2	France	Italy
Scorers		
June 6	Argentina	France
Scorers		
June 6	Italy	Hungary
Scorers		
June 10	Italy	Argentina
Scorers		
June 10	France	Hungary
Scorers		

Final table	P	W	D	L	F	A	Pts
A1							
B5							

GROUP TWO

June 1	W.Germany	Poland
Scorers		
June 2	Tunisia	Mexico
Scorers		
June 6	Poland	Tunisia
Scorers		
June 6	Mexico	W.Germany
Scorers		
June 10	Mexico	Poland
Scorers		
June 10	Tunisia	W.Germany
Scorers		

Final table	P	W	D	L	F	A	Pts
B6							
A2							

GROUP THREE

June 3	Spain	Austria
Scorers		
June 3	Sweden	Brazil
Scorers		
June 7	Austria	Sweden
Scorers		
June 7	Brazil	Spain
Scorers		
June 11	Sweden	Spain
Scorers		
June 11	Brazil	Austria
Scorers		

Final table	P	W	D	L	F	A	Pts
A3							
B7							

GROUP FOUR

June 3	Peru	Scotland
Scorers		
June 3	Iran	Holland
Scorers		
June 7	Scotland	Iran
Scorers		
June 7	Holland	Peru
Scorers		
June 11	Peru	Iran
Scorers		
June 11	Scotland	Holland
Scorers		

Final table	P	W	D	L	F	A	Pts
B8							
A4							

SECOND SERIES

GROUP A

June 14	A2	A1
Scorers		
June 14	A3	A4
Scorers		
June 18	A1	A3
Scorers		
June 18	A4	A2
Scorers		
June 21	A4	A1
Scorers		
June 21	A3	A2
Scorers		

Final table	P	W	D	L	F	A	Pts

GROUP B

June 14	B6	B5
Scorers		
June 14	B7	B8
Scorers		
June 18	B5	B7
Scorers		
June 18	B8	B6
Scorers		
June 21	B8	B5
Scorers		
June 21	B7	B6
Scorers		

Final table	P	W	D	L	F	A	Pts

THE 18-carat gold World Cup, stands approximately 20 inches high and weighs some 11lb. It replaced the Jules Rimet Trophy, won outright by Brazil after their third victory in 1970 in Mexico.

THIRD PLACE PLAY-OFF

June 24, Buenos Aires

Scorers:

Scorers:

WORLD CUP FINAL

June 25, Buenos Aires

Scorers:

Scorers:

ABOVE: President Videla eyes the ultimate prize.

BELOW: English participation was limited to Stuart Pearson wishing Rainer Bonhof best luck following West Germany's warm-up friendly against England in February 1978.

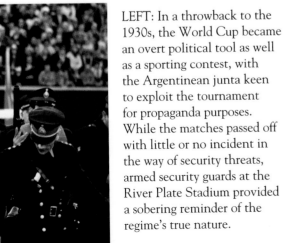

LEFT: In a throwback to the 1930s, the World Cup became an overt political tool as well as a sporting contest, with the Argentinean junta keen to exploit the tournament for propaganda purposes. While the matches passed off with little or no incident in the way of security threats, armed security guards at the River Plate Stadium provided a sobering reminder of the regime's true nature.

LEFT: With sponsors logos to the fore, 1958 Golden Boot winner Just Fontaine does some leg work.

In 1974 the Scots had departed with good wishes but little in the way of real expectation on the part of their supporters. Four years later, the mood was more confident, invigorated by manager Ally MacLeod's startling, if perhaps tongue-in-cheek claim, that his side would win the cup. Having beaten England 2-1 at Wembley in 1977 hopes were magnified even further, and, in a special event at Hampden Park, a huge crowd gave the squad a tumultuous send off.

Ally's Tartan Army

"
Interviewer: "What will you do after the World Cup?"
Ally MacLeod: "Retain it."
"

ABOVE: Once again the sole British team to qualify, Scotland, were pursued by the media. Music superstar and Scotland fan Rod Stewart called in on the squad at their headquarters to bid them luck and cut a record with the players called 'Ole Ola'. Left to right: Kenny Dalglish, Rod Stewart and Sandy Jardine.

ABOVE: Also heading into the studio was Andy Cameron to record 'Ally's Tartan Army', which featured the memorable lines "We're representing Britain, And we're gaunny do or die, England cannae dae it, 'Cos they didnae qualify!"

LEFT: Colourful yarns are spun to this day of how Scotland fans managed to get to Argentina – there are even claims that a group travelled by submarine. Charlie Gibbons and Alistair Steele made their way by more conventional means, including bus.

Kilt-wearing Denis Law was also Argentine-bound, though this time as pundit for the BBC.

Cubillas the Tormentor

With 14 minutes gone in Cordoba, Joe Jordan (right) had given Scotland the lead in their opening Group 4 game and the expected victory over Peru looked to be in the bag. Calamity soon struck, however, and in little over an hour, Scotland's campaign was left hanging in the balance.

RIGHT: Substitute Graeme Souness was in assured mood before kick-off.

Teófilo Cubillas (above) became one of the stars of the tournament and was Scotland's tormentor in chief, scoring twice in five second-half minutes as the South Americans stormed back to win 3-1. The first was with a curling free kick struck with the outside of his right foot, the second a long-range effort that left goalkeeper Alan Rough stranded and Cubillas jubilant.

ABOVE: Don Masson's penalty miss in the first half proved crucial.

LEFT: The Peruvian goalkeeper Ramón Quiroga was held aloft in acknowledgement of his penalty save.

To compound the misery, Willie Johnston, seen here distraught at Scottish HQ, failed a mandatory drugs test after the Peru game and was sent home. To this day Johnston is adamant he took nothing more narcotic than a medicine for hay fever. An exasperated Ally MacLeod grabbed every pill the squad had and threw them into a field.

Worse was to come. Scotland could only draw 1-1 with lowly Iran in their next game (below inset), leaving the side needing a miracle to qualify. The Tartan Army Scottish fans vented their anger.

ABOVE: MacLeod felt the press-conference pressure.

Scotland's Last Hurrah

Beating the 1974 runners-up, the Netherlands, who were building up a nice head of steam as they attempted a second consecutive appearance in the final, was always going to be a tough task. Needing a three-goal winning margin to qualify ahead of the Dutch made it a near impossibility. Yet, with what was arguably their finest ever World Cup performance, Scotland so nearly achieved a miracle.

RIGHT: After Joe Jordan had struck the bar and Kenny Dalglish (left) had had a goal disallowed, the Dutch took the lead through Rensenbrink's penalty. Dalglish gave the Scots a deserved equalizer a minute before half-time.

LEFT: As he and his team-mates strained every sinew, Souness was upended, with Dutch keeper Jan Jongbloed collecting the ball from the feet of his captain Ruud Krol.

RESULTADO FINAL

ESCOCIA 3 HOLANDA 2

CORDOBA

2

PERU 4 IRAN 1

9 0

STEWART - WARNER   AUTOTROL

The fairytale was over. Johnny Rep's 25-yarder, unleashed just three minutes after Gemmill's wonder goal, meant Scotland went out on goal difference. In the post-mortem, MacLeod was suitably vilified for his over-confidence, but in view of Scotland's meek World Cup performances since, his optimism stands as a rare moment when the country could dream the dream.

An image that still brings tears to the eyes of grown Scotsmen. After giving his side the lead two minutes into the second half from the penalty spot, Archie Gemmill weaved his way into his nation's and World Cup folklore with one of the competition's finest solo goals. Picking the ball up on the right wing, Gemmill jinked past three defenders before lofting a measured chip over Jongbloed and into the net. 3-1 and it was game on – Scotland needed just one more goal to pull off their greatest ever result.

Making his World Cup debut for an emerging France team was future UEFA President Michel Platini, though he could do little to prevent his team exiting the competition from a tough opening group featuring Argentina and Italy.

Italy benefited from big support thanks to a large immigrant population in Argentina.

No need for metal fences at Argentinean stadiums, as illustrated by this fearsome moat at the Mar Del Plata ground.

Drum majorettes added an incongruous splash of American razzle-dazzle during half-time in Italy's 2-1 victory over France.

Brazil again reached the third place playoff for the second World Cup in a row but, as in 1974, struggled to emulate the glorious heights of the 1970 side. The most notable contributions to the tournament's history were two superb long-range goals from Nelinho (right), registered in the second phase win over Poland and the playoff victory against Italy. Not forgetting an extraordinary incident in the Group 3 1-1 draw with Sweden: into injury time, Nelinho swung over a corner for Zico to head home the winner – but referee Clive Thomas had blown for full time with the ball in flight before Zico scored. Despite furious protests, Thomas had no doubts.

LEFT: Four European teams made up Group A in the second phase, and they effectively cancelled each other out, with two draws and only one victory by more than a single goal in the six matches. The holders and Italy could only draw 0-0. For Italy, however, managed by Enzo Bearzot and led by Dino Zoff (shaking hands with Berti Vogts), their fourth-place finish suggested better times to come.

ABOVE: Italy had inflicted a 1-0 defeat on Argentina in the first group stage, but the hosts recovered to reach the final. The crunch tie came in the final Group B game with Peru. Needing a four-goal winning margin to ensure they finished above arch-rivals Brazil, Argentina thumped Peru 6-0 – a shock score line considering the winners had only scored six goals in all their previous games and Peru had only conceded a total of six in theirs. Given the political situation in the country at the time, with the junta desperate for a World Cup victory, and that Peru's keeper Quiroga was actually Argentinean, there have been mutterings ever since that the game was fixed, even including claims of involvement by Colombian drug barons. Whatever the truth – and there has been no proof of any collusion – Argentina had booked their place with destiny.

LEFT: Argentina's Leopoldo Luque sported a black eye two days before the final. His form had waned after the injury and death of his brother in a car crash, but he still scored twice in the victory over Peru.

131

Ossie Ardiles

Mario Kempes and Alberto Luque grabbed the media attention for their goals and flowing locks; Daniel Passarella was an inspirational captain. But the tireless heartbeat of the Argentinean side was a diminutive midfielder whose ceaseless running and intelligent distribution from the centre of midfield laid the foundation for the South Americans' famous victory. Ossie Ardiles transformed English football in a 10-year career at Spurs in the aftermath of the 1978 World Cup, and the tournament provided a showcase for his talents. Despite carrying an injury, Ardiles probed and prompted with typical energy in the final. The build-up to Kempes' opening goal was a prime example. His darting run through the midfield, holding off a string of Dutch players before feeding a pass to Luque, who in turn released Kempes, perfectly illustrated Ardiles' strength, balance and awareness.

Ardiles was a kindred spirit of manager César Luis Menotti. So closely did coach and player identify with each other in terms of philosophy and approach that team-mates joshed that he was "son of Menotti". The 1978 final, against the side that embodied the Total Football style Ardiles so admired, was the shining high point in both men's careers.

RIGHT: César Luis Menotti, Ardiles' mentor.

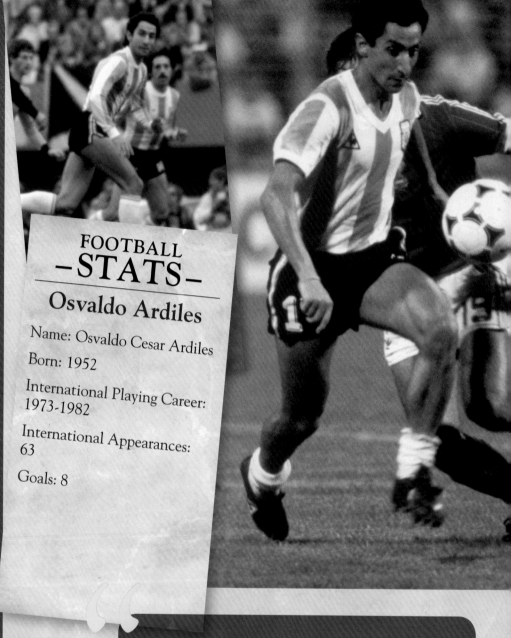

FOOTBALL
–STATS–
Osvaldo Ardiles

Name: Osvaldo Cesar Ardiles

Born: 1952

International Playing Career: 1973-1982

International Appearances: 63

Goals: 8

Before joy, ecstasy or elation I felt relief, that we had done what we had set out to do.

Ossie Ardiles, on the World Cup triumph

The Final

Outside the imposing River Plate Stadium, which was the 72,000-capacity venue for the final, expectant Argentinean fans gathered, including this supporter well prepared for rain.

> *We are one step away from glory.*
>
> César Luis Menotti

And the band played on...

After a month of intense competition, this was what the World Cup had boiled down to – the most cherished prize in team sport. For Argentina the match was a poignant one. During a dark period in their country's history, the World Cup provided a unity of sorts for the people, and relief from the repression of the time. The grim realities of military rule meant that, just a mile away from the stadium, political dissidents were being tortured in the Naval Mechanics School, a notorious centre where many of the thousands of people who "disappeared" during the junta regime were murdered.

The Netherlands dominated the second half and finally equalized in the 82nd minute through Dick Nanninga. Robbie Rensenbrink (above, flat on his back) almost won it right at the death, but his shot hit the post.

Many neutrals favoured the Dutch, believing that their brand of football deserved to win football's ultimate honour. They had beaten Italy 2-1 in the final second phase game and looked to be hitting peak form at just the right time, with Arie Haan in long-range goal-scoring form. There was controversy, however, before the final had even kicked off. Having already kept the Dutch waiting on the pitch before they entered the arena, Argentina complained about the plaster cast René van der Kerkhof had on his injured wrist. If the delay was intended as some kind of mind game, it worked, with the hosts starting the stronger and taking the lead through Kempes in the 38th minute.

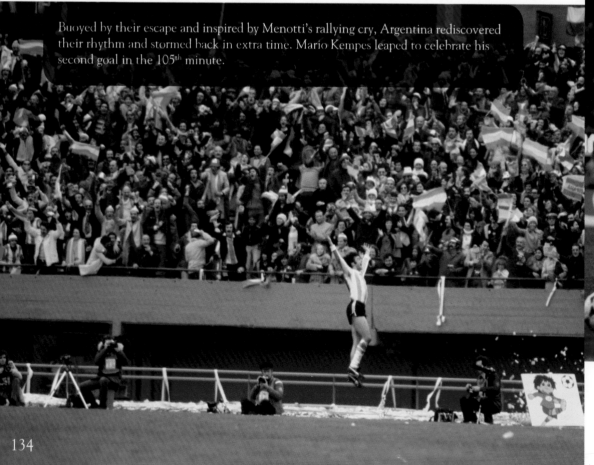

Buoyed by their escape and inspired by Menotti's rallying cry, Argentina rediscovered their rhythm and stormed back in extra time. Mario Kempes leaped to celebrate his second goal in the 105th minute.

ABOVE: Daniel Bertoni wrapped up the win with Argentina's third, four minutes from the final whistle.

134

LEFT: Luque, Kempes and Bertoni joined together in victory.

BELOW LEFT & RIGHT: Bertoni (left) and Jan Poortvliet (right) summed up the contrasting emotions of winners and losers. The brilliant Dutch had once again been denied at the last, and to date, World Cup glory is still to elude them.

Argentina supporters celebrate their country's famous win, 25th June 1978, River Plate Stadium, Buenos Aires.

Italy's Hat-Trick Triumph
1982

The 1982 World Cup final in Madrid's Bernabeu Stadium, and having taken an unassailable lead, Italy's Claudio Gentile (No. 6) and team-mates celebrate a memorable win.

Perugia's draw with Avellino in Italy's Serie A on **30th December 1979** almost turned the course of World Cup history. The game was caught up in a betting scandal that implicated a number of players including Perugia's Paolo Rossi and led to a three-year ban for the striker, commuted to two years – just in time for Rossi to play in the 1982 finals. Defeat to the Soviet Union on **18th November 1981** meant that Wales just failed to join England, Scotland and Northern Ireland in a repeat of 1958 when all four home nations qualified for the finals. For the first time two African teams – Algeria and Cameroon – qualified to take part after Cameroon's African 4th Group stage win against Morocco on **29th November 1981**. A new format was introduced: there were still two qualifying phases but straight knockout semi-finals made a welcome return. The number of competing teams rose from 16 to 24. On **2nd April 1982**, Argentina's invasion of the Falklands ignited war with Britain and threatened to derail possible fixtures between the South Americans and the home nations. The tournament began on **13th June** with a surprise 1-0 defeat for holders Argentina by Belgium. Algeria beat West Germany 2-1 on **16th June** in the first major shock of the tournament. On **17th June**, at the age of 17 and 41 days, Norman Whiteside became the youngest player in World Cup history, beating Pelé's record set in 1958. Italy's draw with Cameroon on **23rd June** meant the eventual winners qualified for the next phase having not won a single first-stage game.

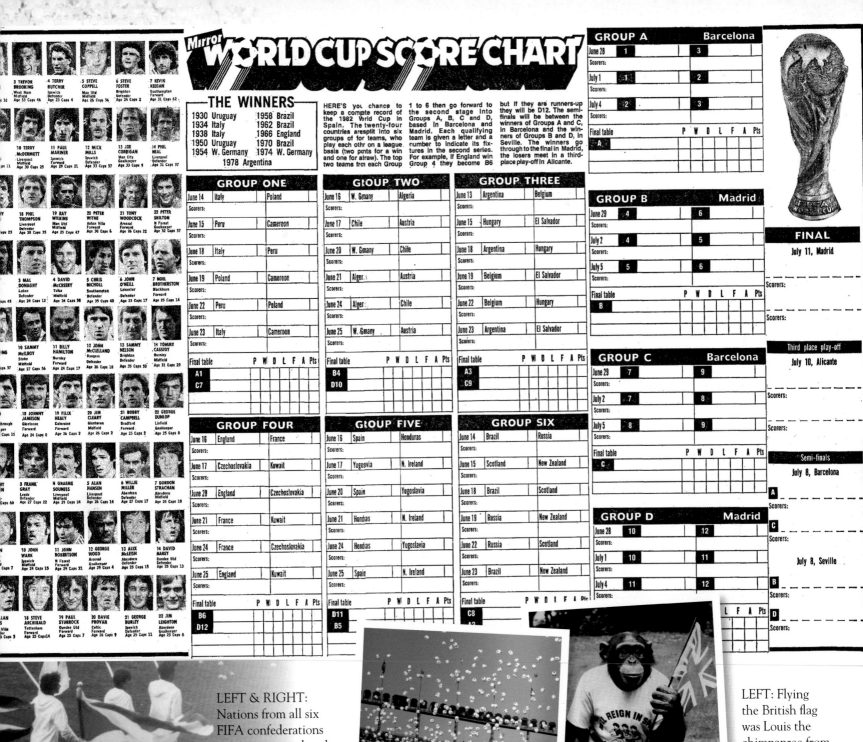

Mirror WORLD CUP SCORE CHART

Player headshots (left column):

3 TREVOR BROOKING – West Ham, Midfield, Age 33 Caps 46
4 TERRY BUTCHER – Ipswich, Defender, Age 23 Caps 4
5 STEVE COPPELL – Man Utd, Midfield, Age 26 Caps 36
6 STEVE FOSTER – Brighton, Defender, Age 24 Caps 3
7 KEVIN KEEGAN – Southampton, Forward, Age 31 Caps 62

10 TERRY McDERMOTT – Liverpool, Midfield, Age 30 Caps 25
11 PAUL MARINER – Ipswich, Forward, Age 29 Caps 21
12 MICK MILLS – Ipswich, Defender, Age 33 Caps 9
13 JOE CORRIGAN – Man City, Goalkeeper, Age 33 Caps 9
14 PHIL NEAL – Liverpool, Defender, Age 31 Caps 42

18 PHIL THOMPSON – Liverpool, Defender, Age 28 Caps 35
19 RAY WILKINS – Man Utd, Midfield, Age 25 Caps 47
20 PETER WITHE – Aston Villa, Forward, Age 30 Caps 6
21 TONY WOODCOCK – Arsenal, Forward, Age 26 Caps 22
22 PETER SHILTON – N Forest, Goalkeeper, Age 32 Caps 37

3 MAL DONAGHY – Luton, Defender, Age 24 Caps 12
4 DAVID McCREERY – Tulsa, Midfield, Age 24 Caps 44
5 CHRIS NICHOLL – Southampton, Defender, Age 35 Caps 40
6 JOHN O'NEILL – Leicester, Defender, Age 23 Caps 17
7 NOEL BROTHERSTON – Blackburn, Forward, Age 25 Caps 16

10 SAMMY McILROY – Stoke, Midfield, Age 27 Caps 56
11 BILLY HAMILTON – Burnley, Forward, Age 24 Caps 17
12 JOHN McCLELLAND – Rangers, Defender, Age 26 Caps 18
13 SAMMY NELSON – Brighton, Defender, Age 35 Caps 50
14 TOMMY CASSIDY – Burnley, Midfield, Age 31 Caps 23

18 JOHNNY JAMESON – Glentoran, Forward, Age 24 Caps 0
19 FELIX HEALY – Coleraine, Forward, Age 26 Caps 2
20 JIM CLEARY – Glentoran, Midfield, Age 26 Caps 2
21 BOBBY CAMPBELL – Bradford, Forward, Age 25 Caps 8
22 GEORGE DUNLOP – Linfield, Goalkeeper, Age 25 Caps 0

3 FRANK GRAY – Leeds, Defender, Age 27 Caps 24
4 GRAEME SOUNESS – Liverpool, Midfield, Age 29 Caps 24
5 ALAN HANSEN – Liverpool, Defender, Age 26 Caps 14
6 WILLIE MILLER – Aberdeen, Defender, Age 27 Caps 17
7 GORDON STRACHAN – Aberdeen, Midfield, Age 25 Caps 10

10 JOHN WARK – Ipswich, Midfield, Age 24 Caps 15
11 JOHN ROBERTSON – N Forest, Forward, Age 29 Caps 21
12 GEORGE WOOD – Arsenal, Goalkeeper, Age 29 Caps 4
13 ALEX McLEISH – Aberdeen, Defender, Age 23 Caps 15
14 DAVID NAREY – Dundee Utd, Defender, Age 25 Caps 13

18 STEVE ARCHIBALD – Tottenham, Forward, Age 25 Caps14
19 PAUL STURROCK – Dundee Utd, Forward, Age 25 Caps 7
20 DAVIE PROVAN – Celtic, Forward, Age 26 Caps 9
21 GEORGE BURLEY – Ipswich, Defender, Age 25 Caps 11
22 JIM LEIGHTON – Aberdeen, Goalkeeper, Age 23 Caps 6

THE WINNERS

1930	Uruguay	1958	Brazil
1934	Italy	1962	Brazil
1938	Italy	1966	England
1950	Uruguay	1970	Brazil
1954	W. Germany	1974	W. Germany
	1978	Argentina	

HERE'S your chance to keep a complete record of the 1982 World Cup in Spain. The twenty-four countries are split into six groups of four teams, who play each other on a league basis (two points for a win and one for a draw). The top two teams from each Group 1 to 6 then go forward to the second stage into Groups A, B, C and D, based in Barcelona and Madrid. Each qualifying team is given a letter and a number to indicate its fixtures in the second series. For example, if England win Group 4 they become B6 but if they are runners-up they will be D12. The semi-finals will be between the winners of Groups A and C, in Barcelona and the winners of Groups B and D, in Seville. The winners go through to the final in Madrid, the losers meet in a third-place play-off in Alicante.

GROUP ONE

June 14	Italy	Poland
June 15	Peru	Cameroon
June 18	Italy	Peru
June 19	Poland	Cameroon
June 22	Peru	Poland
June 23	Italy	Cameroon

Final table — P W D L F A Pts
A1
C7

GROUP TWO

June 16	W. Germany	Algeria
June 17	Chile	Austria
June 20	W. Germany	Chile
June 21	Algeria	Austria
June 24	Algeria	Chile
June 25	W. Germany	Austria

Final table — P W D L F A Pts
B4
D10

GROUP THREE

June 13	Argentina	Belgium
June 15	Hungary	El Salvador
June 18	Argentina	Hungary
June 19	Belgium	El Salvador
June 22	Belgium	Hungary
June 23	Argentina	El Salvador

Final table — P W D L F A Pts
A3
C9

GROUP FOUR

June 16	England	France
June 17	Czechoslovakia	Kuwait
June 20	England	Czechoslovakia
June 21	France	Kuwait
June 24	France	Czechoslovakia
June 25	England	Kuwait

Final table — P W D L F A Pts
B6
D12

GROUP FIVE

June 16	Spain	Honduras
June 17	Yugoslavia	N. Ireland
June 20	Spain	Yugoslavia
June 21	Honduras	N. Ireland
June 24	Honduras	Yugoslavia
June 25	Spain	N. Ireland

Final table — P W D L F A Pts
D11
B5

GROUP SIX

June 14	Brazil	Russia
June 15	Scotland	New Zealand
June 18	Brazil	Scotland
June 19	Russia	New Zealand
June 22	Russia	Scotland
June 23	Brazil	New Zealand

Final table — P W D L F A Pts
C8

GROUP A — Barcelona

June 28	1	3
July 1	1	2
July 4	2	3

Final table — P W D L F A Pts
A

GROUP B — Madrid

June 29	4	6
July 2	4	5
July 5	5	6

Final table — P W D L F A Pts
B

GROUP C — Barcelona

June 29	7	9
July 2	7	8
July 5	8	9

Final table — P W D L F A Pts
C

GROUP D — Madrid

June 28	10	12
July 1	10	11
July 4	11	12

Final table — P W D L F A Pts
D

FINAL
July 11, Madrid
Scorers:

Third place play-off
July 10, Alicante
Scorers:

Semi-finals
July 8, Barcelona
A
C
Scorers:

July 8, Seville
B
D
Scorers:

LEFT & RIGHT: Nations from all six FIFA confederations were represented at the opening ceremony.

LEFT: Flying the British flag was Louis the chimpanzee from Twycross Zoo.

Brits Abroad

With three sides in the competition, the UK had its most significant presence at the World Cup since 1958. The surprise was that Northern Ireland, the most unfancied of the trio, made the biggest impact.

Northern Ireland were placed in a tough group that included hosts Spain and Yugoslavia. They got off to a good start after a 0-0 draw against the Balkans, with 17-year-old Norman Whiteside causing problems for the Yugoslav rearguard.

ABOVE: While Gerry Armstrong (with a couple of Spanish police at the team's HQ) was a decent enough striker for Spurs, Watford and Brighton, he was hardly a household name in Britain, still less so in international circles. Yet he and his team-mates made their mark on the World Cup in wonderful fashion. After a 1-1 draw with Honduras, Northern Ireland needed to beat Spain to make it to the next round. They were given few chances, but Armstrong pounced on a mistake by goalkeeper Arconada to secure a remarkable victory.

A 2-2 draw in the Group 4 second-phase game against Austria, with Billy Hamilton scoring twice, encouraged Irish hopes even further, but a 4-1 reverse to an improving French side (with 37-year-old Pat Jennings in goal) finally brought the fairytale to an end.

Northern Ireland
supporters and players
made quite an impression.

LEFT & ABOVE: In contrast to other sides that locked themselves away in aloof seclusion, Northern Ireland relaxed and enjoyed the moment. Armstrong and Pat Jennings took it easy in the shade, while pictured enjoying a drink were (left to right) Chris Nicholl, John McLelland, Billy Hamilton, John O'Neill and Bobby Campbell.

BELOW: O'Neill was joined by fiancée Mary Duffy as well as Nicholl and his wife Jenny.

There were no grand claims of winning the World Cup this time around for Scotland, but the Group 6 draw did Jock Stein's side no favours. New Zealand were brushed aside 5-2, but heavy defeat to a quite brilliant Brazil team, followed up with an error-strewn draw with the Soviet Union meant Scotland were out within a fortnight.

In the encounter with Brazil, Scotland took a surprise but merited lead thanks to David Narey's long-range strike.

The South Americans soon hit back, and in some style. Zico's free kick left Alan Rough (left) with no chance, before Oscar's header, Falcão's late low drive and, best of all, Eder's imperious chip, completed the rout. It was no disgrace, however, to lose 4-1 to such an outstanding team.

Gordon Strachan in action during the 5-2 win, Scotland's biggest ever victory in the World Cup.

John Wark in action for Scotland against the Soviets.

Needing a win over the Soviets to make it into the next round, Scotland took the lead but were undone by some calamitous defending, chiefly when a mix-up between Alan Hansen and Willie Miller allowed Ramaz Shengelia (below, with Miller) through to give the Soviets the lead. Graeme Souness' fine equalizer was not enough, and Scotland were out.

For the Tartan Army, witnessing brave but doomed World Cup performances was becoming a familiar experience.

On the country's return to World Cup centre-stage for the first time in 12 years, England's prospects were, as ever, talked up beyond the side's true capabilities. While Ron Greenwood's players qualified for the second phase and remained unbeaten, they were no match for the genuinely world-class outfits, and were burdened by a struggle to create opportunities and score goals.

FAR LEFT: Greenwood was a highly rated and safe pair of hands as manager, bringing stability to the role after Don Revie's short but troubled tenure. He could call on the likes of £1million-man Trevor Francis (seated on ground), but his job at the World Cup was made difficult by injuries to two of his better players, Trevor Brooking and Kevin Keegan (inset).

England could not have got off to a better start. Bryan Robson's goal after 27 seconds against France, beating past French goalkeeper Jean-Luc Ettori, was then the fastest in World Cup history. Robson received an inscribed Seiko watch for the feat.

France were eventually beaten 3-1 with Paul Mariner (below) scoring the third. Further victories over Czechoslovakia and Kuwait hinted at exciting promise, but in the second qualifying group successive goalless draws with Germany and Spain ended England's participation.

RIGHT: Greenwood cast caution aside only at the last, risking Keegan and Brooking as substitutes in pursuit of a vital goal against Spain with 26 minutes to go of their contest in Madrid. Keegan, however, wasted a glorious opportunity by heading wide with one of England's few clear chances.

Commiserations all round but Spain and England were out.

Away from the disappointments on the pitch England players did their best to enjoy themselves.

When in Basque country, wear a Basque hat.

ABOVE: Such were the security concerns caused by the Falklands conflict that armed guards were present at training.

LEFT: Life's a beach for the partners of Messrs Samson, Hoddle and Rix.

'The English Disease'

Sadly, the 1982 World Cup will also be known for the time when hooliganism became a feature of the tournament. Violent England fans had been involved in serious disorder at a number of fixtures in previous years, and Spanish security forces were on high, and perhaps over-zealous, alert.

Guards pointed out possible troublemakers during the England–France game.

England followers were also on the receiving end, as the injuries on these two supporters vividly illustrated.

ABOVE & BELOW: Crowd trouble was, thankfully, an isolated occurrence. England fans travelled to Spain in large numbers and, whether sleeping on the beach or fraternizing with the law, most came for the football experience and not the punch-ups.

West German fans were also the subject of police attention, as in this 4-1 Group 2 win

Fans United

With 24 nations from six continents taking part, Spain '82 welcomed visitors from a range of footballing cultures.

Divine intervention from one Peru fan.

Kuwaitis gleefully expressed their patriotism.

ABOVE: West German supporters were present in large numbers in Spain.

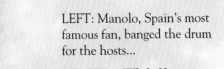
LEFT: Manolo, Spain's most famous fan, banged the drum for the hosts...

BELOW: ...While King Juan Carlos was one very important spectator.

The Samba Boys from Brazil

For many people who watched the 1982 World Cup, the Brazil side managed by Tele Santana (inset) were not just the team of the tournament, they were one of *the* best teams in World Cup history. For certain, there have been winners who do not come close to the '82 vintage in terms of skill, flair and artistry, expressed by a team packed with individual brilliance. By rights they should have won the World Cup at a canter, but their defensive flaws, and Italy's determination not to play the role of whipping boys, exposed an inability to defend a 2-2 scoreline that would have seen them through to the semi-finals. Nonetheless, a gallery of great players left a marvellous legacy.

Socrates

Junior

A chain-smoking political activist and doctor of philosophy who once played for Garforth Town in the English Northern Counties League, Socrates (right) was the conductor of Brazil's orchestra. Having notched a stupendous goal against the USSR he taught the young Maradona a goal-scoring lesson from midfield in Brazil's 3-1 win over Argentina, aided by the mercurial Falcão (left), who himself smashed two goals from distance in the games against Scotland and Italy.

Junior was the team's best defender but was masterful in the role of attacking full-back, scoring a tremendous goal against Argentina.

Eder

Zico

Eder was the maverick of the side, prone to occasionally infuriating behaviour on and off the pitch, but capable of producing moments of sheer footballing beauty. Eder made good goalkeepers look stupid: his sublime chipped goal against the helpless Alan Rough in the defeat of Scotland was surpassed only by the goal of the tournament in the defeat of the USSR, when he juggled the ball on his left before unleashing an outrageous, thunderous volley that left Rinat Dassayev rooted to the spot.

Between 1978 and 1986, Zico was one of the world's most acclaimed players. His outstanding performances and goals made him one of the undoubted stars of 1982, whether with an acrobatic bicycle kick and goal against New Zealand, a belting free-kick inflicted upon Scotland, or the lightning quick turn and pass that set up Socrates for his own dramatic goal against Italy.

–STAR–
OF THE TOURNAMENT

Paolo Rossi

Having come into the tournament just freed from a ban stemming from a corruption scandal in Italy in which he has denied involvement, and without a goal to his name in the first four games, it appeared that Paolo Rossi was not destined to enjoy the happiest of World Cups. Yet, by the end, he had the unique distinction of being top scorer, player of the tournament and a World Cup winner's medal around his neck. Repaying the faith of manager Enzo Bearzot, Rossi had suddenly hit peak form, scoring three goals in the standout match against Brazil. His predatory instincts were never better illustrated than with his hat-trick goal, pouncing on the loose ball to turn and rifle home. It was the key moment in the 1982 World Cup, ending Brazil's participation and providing momentum for an improving Italian side timing their run to the final to perfection.

A European Cup winner with Juventus in 1985, he travelled with the national side to Mexico in 1986 but took no part in the defence of the trophy. His World Cup impact may have thus been a relatively brief one, but it was one of the most significant in the competition's history.

FOOTBALL –STATS–
Paolo Rossi

Name: Paolo Rossi

Born: 1956

International Playing Career: 1977-1986

International Appearances: 48

Goals: 20

Rossi failed to get on the scoresheet during the Group 3 game against Argentina but thereafter began to show the form that would transform his World Cup.

Italy manager Enzo Bearzot was rewarded for keeping faith with Rossi.

Enzo Bearzot believed in me and was sure I would come through at the right time.

Paolo Rossi

The on-fire Rossi scored twice against Poland in the semis to secure Italy's passage to the final. The Poles were missing their most effective player, Zbigniew Boniek, due to suspension, and could not contain an increasingly effective Italian team.

LEFT: In the other semi-final, a workmanlike West German side had managed to win through after a round of group games distinguished only by the suspect 1-0 win over Austria. Knowing such a score would see both sides through, the teams played out an insipid match that resembled more of a training session than a World Cup encounter, and enabled the Germanic neighbours to progress at Algeria's expense. The resulting outcry led to a change in the rules whereby such deciding games had to kick off at the same time.

West Germany now faced France, the antithesis of Jupp Derwall's side in their commitment to free-flowing football, exemplified by captain Michel Platini (inset). But the result did not go France's way. After West Germany's Harald Schumacher (left) had taken out Patrick Battiston with a dreadful late challenge, the unpunished keeper and his team-mates won a memorable game on penalties, having clawed back a 3-1 French lead to draw 3-3 after extra time.

157

An ecstatic Rossi is a picture of joy unconfined as he celebrates the decisive goal in the 3-1 win over the Germans, scored by Alessandro Altobelli (No. 18). Rossi's 57th-minute opener, and Marco Tardelli's second 12 minutes later had given Italy a 2-0 lead, with Paul Breitner's strike a minute from time the barest of consolations.

Italy may not have had the flair of Brazil or France, but with talents such as Bruno Conti, Francesco Graziani, Giancarlo Antognoni, Claudio Gentile and Antonio Cabrini they were a well-balanced side, led by the shining example of 40-year-old Dino Zoff.

BELOW: Zoff and Italy victorious.

Argentina's Divine Intervention
1986

Peter Shilton shakes hands with Diego Maradona before kick-off in the epic quarter-final between England and Argentina. It was Maradona's hand and his supreme skill that were to provide the defining moments of the 1986 World Cup.

The 13th World Cup was due to take place in Colombia, but a worsening political situation forced the country to withdraw in **November 1982** and the honour instead went to Mexico, which thus became the first nation to hold the event twice. Echoing the natural disaster of the 1962 tournament in Chile, an earthquake struck Mexico in **September 1985**, killing over 10,000 and leading to concerns the tournament might be in jeopardy. Scotland's 1-1 qualifying phase draw with Wales ended in tragedy with the death at 62 of manager Jock Stein, who suffered a heart attack shortly after his team had scored; Alex Ferguson later took over as boss. The 0-0 draw between England and Northern Ireland on **13th November 1985** ensured both nations qualified for Mexico '86. Iraq's 3-1 victory over Syria on **29th November** completed their successful qualifying campaign. All their home games were played on neutral territory because of the Iran–Iraq war. At the age of 41, Pat Jennings won the last of his 119 caps in Northern Ireland's 3-0 defeat to Brazil on **12th June 1986**. One minute into the Scotland–Uruguay clash on **13th June**, José Batista set an unenviable record for the fastest sending off in World Cup history after a foul on Gordon Strachan. In-form Denmark took an early lead against Spain in their last-16 meeting on **18th June** only to lose 5-1, with Emilio Butragueño scoring four goals. **21st June** saw the game of the tournament, when France knocked out Brazil 4-3 on penalties after a scintillating 1-1 draw in extra time.

LEFT: In November 1985, England manager Bobby Robson raised a toast for his side's chances in the forthcoming World Cup.

YOUR PULL-OUT & KEEP GUIDE

FIRST ROUND ☆

BRAZIL		June 1. Jalisco KO 7pm
N. IRE	ITV	June 3. 3 de Marzo
ALGERIA		June 6. Jalisco KO 7pm
SPAIN	ITV	June 7. 3 de Marzo
BRAZIL	BBC	June 12. Jalisco KO 7pm
SPAIN		June 12 Tecnológica KO 7pm

D TABLE

P	W	D	L	F	A	Pts

FIRST ROUND ☆

W. GER		June 4. Corregidora KO 7pm
DENMARK	ITV	June 4. Neza '86
SCOTLAND	BBC	June 8. Corregidora KO 7pm
URUGUAY		June 8. Neza '86 KO 11pm
W. GERMANY		June 13. Corregidora KO 7pm
URUGUAY	ITV	June 13. Neza '86 KO 11pm

E TABLE

P	W	D	L	F	A	Pts

FIRST ROUND ☆

POLAND		June 2. Universitario KO 11pm
ENGLAND	BBC	June 3. Tecnológica KO 11pm
MOROCCO	ITV	June 6. Universitario KO 11pm
PORTUGAL		June 7. Universitario KO 11pm
MOROCCO		June 11. 3 de Marzo
POLAND	BBC	June 11. Universitario KO 11pm

F TABLE

P	W	D	L	F	A	Pts

We're off!
The biggest football tournament in the world is under way with 52 games to be played over 30 fabulous days in Mexico. And you can keep your very own record of the drama with our World Cup wallchart.

SECOND ROUND

MATCH No 1 — June 14 Cuahtemoc Stadium KO 11pm

TEAM	Goals		Goals	TEAM
A1		V		C3 or D3 or E3

MATCH No 2 — June 15 Azteca Stadium KO 7pm

TEAM	Goals		Goals	TEAM
F2		V		B2

MATCH No 3 — June 15 Corregidora Stadium KO 7pm

TEAM	Goals		Goals	TEAM
E1		V		D2

MATCH No 4 — June 15 Neza Stadium KO 11pm

TEAM	Goals		Goals	TEAM
C1		V		A3 or B3 or F3

MATCH No 5 — June 16 Jalisco Stadium KO 11pm

TEAM	Goals		Goals	TEAM
D1		V		B3 or E3 or F3

MATCH No 6 — June 17 Olimpico KO 7pm

TEAM	Goals		Goals	TEAM
A2		V		C2

MATCH No 7 — June 17 Universitario KO 11pm

TEAM	Goals		Goals	TEAM
F1		V		E2

MATCH No 8 — June 18 Azteca Stadium KO 11pm

TEAM	Goals		Goals	TEAM
B1		V		A3 or C3 or D3

QUARTER FINALS

MATCH A — June 21 Azteca Stadium KO 7pm

TEAM	Goals		Goals	TEAM
1		V		2

MATCH B — June 22 Cuahtemoc Stadium KO 11pm

TEAM	Goals		Goals	TEAM
3		V		4

MATCH C — June 21 Jalisco Stadium KO 7pm

TEAM	Goals		Goals	TEAM
5		V		6

MATCH D — June 21 Universitario KO 11pm

TEAM	Goals		Goals	TEAM
7		V		8

SEMI FINALS

TEAM	Goals		Goals	TEAM
A		V		B

June 25. Azteca Stadium, KO 11 pm.

TEAM	Goals		Goals	TEAM
C		V		D

June 25. Jalisco Stadium, KO 7 pm.

3rd/4th PLACE

TEAM	Goals	V	Goals	TEAM

June 28. Cuahtemoc Stadium, KO 7 pm.

CROWNING GLORY

THE FINAL

AZTECA JUNE 29

WINNERS MATCH 1   WINNERS MATCH 2
V
SCORERS GOALS SCORERS

1		
2		
3		
4		
5		
6		
7		
8		
9		
10		
11		
SUBS		
KO 7 pm.		

THE CHAMPIONS

ABOVE: Gary Lineker borrowed a policeman's jacket, hat, and truncheon while warming up in Colorado Springs, USA.

BELOW: England's squad was based on a number of players drawn from the same clubs. Everton's Trevor Steven, Peter Reid, Gary Stevens and Gary Lineker flew the flag along with Tottenham's Chris Waddle, Gary Stevens and Glenn Hoddle, who met up with their manager David Pleat in Mexico. Pleat had just been appointed Spurs boss and used the trip to convince Hoddle to remain in North London for the next season.

Fourth Time Unlucky for Scotland

For the fourth tournament in succession, Scotland were drawn in a tough group and faced a struggle to progress. It was not to be, but – as ever – the team and their followers left their distinctive mark.

Singer Rod Stewart and then girlfriend Kelly Emberg joined thousands of other Scotland fans for the crucial qualifying draw with Wales in September 1985.

ABOVE: Models Lorraine Davidson and Karen Flynn showed off Scotland's official World Cup mascot – the imaginatively named "McMex".

LEFT: Veteran commentator Archie MacPherson was heading to Mexico, and was seen off by Spain fans Nino Mazzone (left) and Luis Letelier-Lobos, both staff members at a Glasgow hotel.

164

ABOVE: Scots greys... the Scotland squad, with new stand-in manager Alex Ferguson, in their besuited finest. World Cup songsmith Andy Cameron (inset) prepared for Mexico in his own inimitable way.

LEFT: Ferguson, pictured with assistant Archie Knox while overseeing training in Sante Fe, had answered his country's call in the wake of Jock Stein's untimely death, and steered Scotland through Mexico '86 before taking up the manager's job at Manchester United.

Brothers-in-arms, Ferguson and Graeme Souness enjoyed the Mexico heat, while Charlie Nicholas (right), then the golden boy of Scottish football, took a refreshing drink.

Defeats to Denmark and West Germany effectively ended Scotland's campaign. A 0-0 draw with Uruguay left them bottom and facing the familiar early departure home. This was despite facing 10 men for 89 minutes after José Batista had been sent off for this crude foul on Gordon Strachan.

With a new manager and fresh faces in the squad, England looked towards their campaign with high hopes for success. The prolific form of striker Gary Lineker gave cause for optimism, fresh from a club season with Everton in which he had top-scored in the first division with 30 goals.

Bobby Robson was no deskbound manager and was an active presence on the training ground.

Messing about in the water, Gary Stevens, Kenny Sansom, and Ray Wilkins make a splash.

Shell-suited and booted at the team hotel. Right to left: Terry Butcher, Chris Waddle, and Viv Anderson, the first black player to play for England.

INSET: Bryan Robson and Ray Wilkins take a sun-dappled bike ride. Robson's persistent injury problems were a hindrance to England's chances.

BELOW: A young shoe cleaner polishes Lineker's boots.

ABOVE: England got off to a bad start with a 1-0 defeat to Portugal, in 1986 a side nothing like the force they are now. Kenny Sansom allowed Diamantino to beat him on the right and cross for an unmarked Carlos Manuel to tap in the only goal of the game.

RIGHT: Portugal's manager José Torres could not, understandably, have been any happier.

ABOVE: Matters worsened after a 0-0 draw with lowly Morocco. Robson had come off after just four minutes with a damaged shoulder, and Wilkins was given the captain's armband, but was promptly sent off for throwing the ball at the referee.

England finally clicked into gear with a convincing 3-0 win over Poland, Lineker scoring a fine hat-trick.

LEFT & BELOW: Ecstatic England fans celebrated happily enough behind fences, but Mexican mounted police were taking no chances and galloped into action to head off any potential trouble.

England's high-water mark came with the 3-0 thumping of Paraguay in the last 16 at the Azteca Stadium. Lineker tapped in the first, Peter Beardsley added a second, before a fine move involving Hoddle and Gary Stevens ended with Lineker scoring his fifth goal of the tournament.

Gurning for the press cameras, Lineker was well on his way to challenging for the top goal scorer's Golden Boot.

A toothless Beardsley and Lineker celebrate at the Azteca. The pair were forging what would become one of England's most effective strike partnerships.

For the crunch quarter-final meeting with Argentina, tensions were high on and off the pitch. It was the first fixture between the two nations since the Falklands conflict.

A flag was set on fire high in the stands.

ABOVE: Despite the friction between some supporters, many others met on friendly terms and witnessed a memorable game of football.

LEFT: A group of England fans make their feelings clear.

LEFT: In the build-up to the game, an England World Cup hero shared confidences with a modern Argentinean one.

BELOW: Surrounded by the world's media, Maradona was the player all eyes were focused on.

In the cauldron-like heat of the Azteca, England and Argentina finally came together to settle scores.

Trevor Steven, caught in perfect corner-taking motion.

RIGHT: England's most naturally gifted flair player, Glenn Hoddle evades a tackle. Debate continues to this day about the midfielder who later became manager of the national team. For many he was a talent wasted in an England shirt. Critics of Bobby Robson and his predecessor Ron Greenwood argue that they failed to exploit Hoddle's range of passing and ability on the ball; Hoddle's detractors say his elegant artistry was ill-suited to a team culturally geared for hard-running and commitment. The debate persists, but one fact is undeniable: Bryan Robson, the tireless but injury-prone "captain marvel" around whom the national side was built, earned 90 caps; his contemporary Hoddle just 53.

LEFT: Amid the heat of intense competition, Maradona handed his midfield marker Steve Hodge some ice to help cool down.

RIGHT: After the action ended, Hodge was the recipient of a very famous No. 10 shirt.

Six minutes into the second half came one of the most dramatic and controversial moments in World Cup history. After Hodge had sliced a clearance, Maradona beat Peter Shilton to the ball and knocked it into the net with his left hand. Referee Ali Bennaceur and his assistants failed to spot the blatant infringement and Argentina were 1-0 up.

Maradona leaps for joy to celebrate his handball goal.

Whoever robs a thief gets a 100-year pardon.

Diego Maradona, justifying the goal with reference to the Falklands war

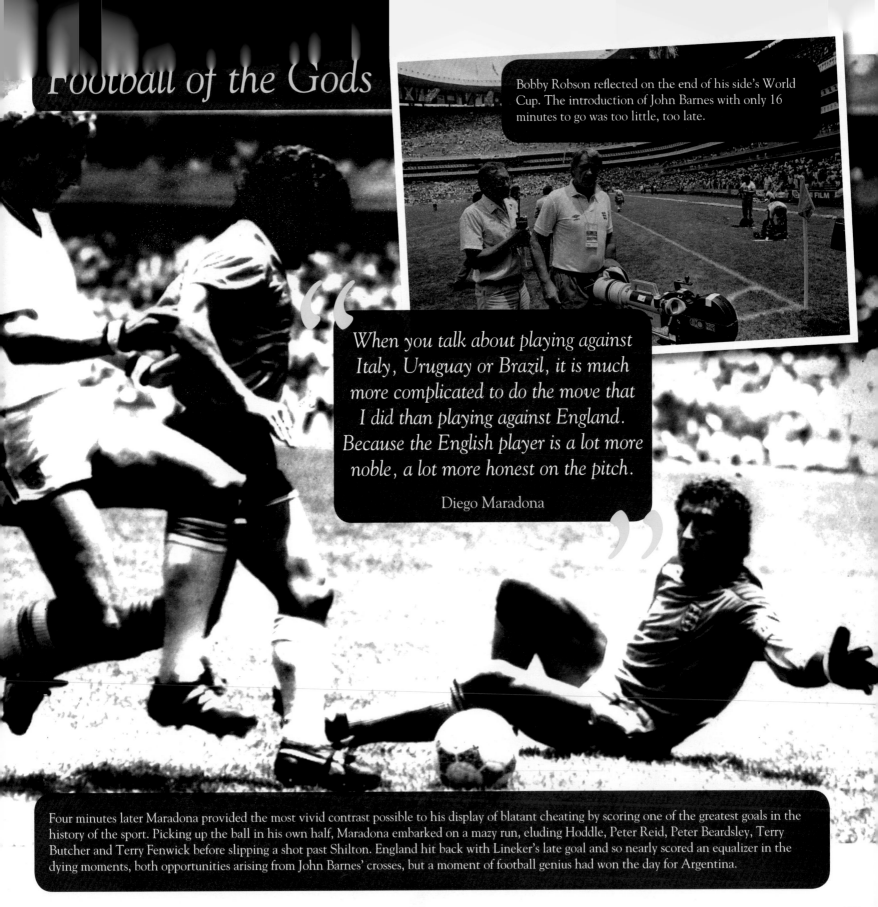

Football of the Gods

Bobby Robson reflected on the end of his side's World Cup. The introduction of John Barnes with only 16 minutes to go was too little, too late.

> "When you talk about playing against Italy, Uruguay or Brazil, it is much more complicated to do the move that I did than playing against England. Because the English player is a lot more noble, a lot more honest on the pitch."
>
> Diego Maradona

Four minutes later Maradona provided the most vivid contrast possible to his display of blatant cheating by scoring one of the greatest goals in the history of the sport. Picking up the ball in his own half, Maradona embarked on a mazy run, eluding Hoddle, Peter Reid, Peter Beardsley, Terry Butcher and Terry Fenwick before slipping a shot past Shilton. England hit back with Lineker's late goal and so nearly scored an equalizer in the dying moments, both opportunities arising from John Barnes' crosses, but a moment of football genius had won the day for Argentina.

—STAR—
OF THE TOURNAMENT

Diego Maradona

Brought up in Buenos Aires not far from the Bombonera Stadium of Boca Juniors, for whom he has always been a fanatical supporter, Diego Maradona has come to embody the extremes of footballing passion. As a player he was almost beyond compare. Short in stature but strong as a bull, he was equipped with extraordinary skills, a bold, fearless attitude and an unquenchable desire to succeed despite the often horrendous physical battering he took from ruthless defenders who could only stop him by illegal means. Though the Argentine 1986 squad had its complement of excellent players, it is difficult to imagine the team would have won the World Cup without Maradona in its ranks.

Idolized around the world, Maradona has even had an Argentinean church founded in his honour. The flip side to his greatness has been a career littered with turmoil, scandal and controversy: cocaine addiction, dismissal from the 1994 World Cup for failing a drugs tests, public rows and a captivating but volatile and impetuous personality that has got him into trouble as much as it has enthralled, mean that Maradona is the definition of a flawed legend.

Tied with Pelé for FIFA's Player of the 20th Century award, his undoubted career high was the 1986 tournament. Indeed, it is arguable that no other player before or since has so stamped his own individual brilliance and character on the competition.

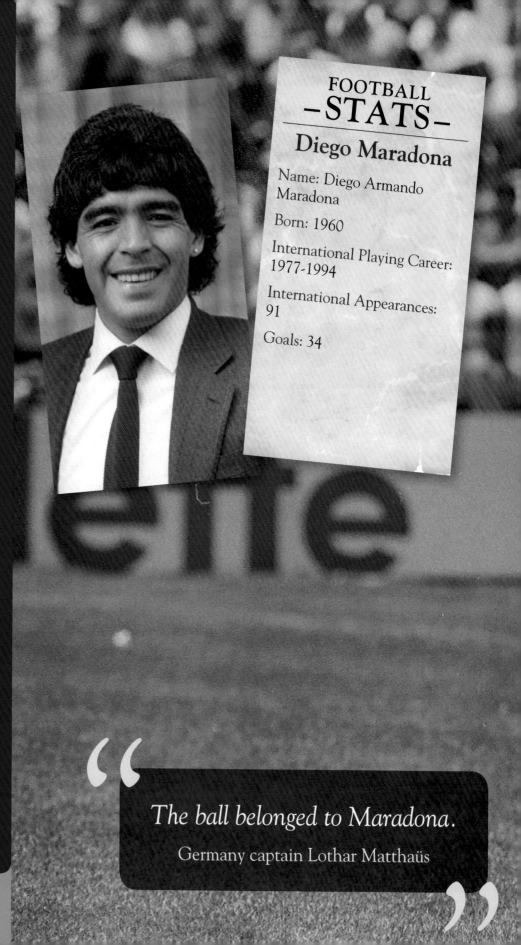

FOOTBALL
—STATS—
Diego Maradona

Name: Diego Armando Maradona

Born: 1960

International Playing Career: 1977-1994

International Appearances: 91

Goals: 34

"
The ball belonged to Maradona.

Germany captain Lothar Matthäus
"

England fans bestow their own unique honour for Maradona at the final whistle of the meeting with Argentina.

WORLD CUP TRIUMPH IS KEY TO FORTUNE FOR MARADONA

THE £10m MAN

MEXICO 86

Diego is dynamite

From HARRY MILLER

DIEGO MARADONA raises the World Cup to celebrate Argentina's victory over West Germany.

After the victory over England, Argentina cast aside Belgium in a semi-final win that featured another unforgettable dribbled goal for Maradona. In the final he and his team-mates faced a West Germany side that was arguably weaker than the team that were runners-up four years earlier. Man-marked by Lothar Matthäus, Maradona was not at his effective finest, but snuffed out the Germans' comeback from two goals down by supplying the pass that released Jorge Burruchaga to score the decisive third goal. In all, Maradona either scored or created 10 of Argentina's goals during the finals.

England's World of Emotion
1990

Consoled by Steve McMahon with an injured Mark Wright, West Germany's Rudi Voller and a tracksuited John Barnes nearby, England's Paul Gascoigne (No. 19) sobs his way into the nation's affections after one of the most dramatic of World Cup semi-finals. The game proved to be a turning point in the fortunes of English football, particularly at club level.

After a disastrous European Championships campaign in **June 1988**, England manager Bobby Robson's offer to resign was rejected by the FA. During the South American Zone Group 3 qualifying match when Brazil led Chile 1-0 on **3rd September 1989**, Chilean goalkeeper Roberto Rojas pretended to be struck by a firework thrown onto the pitch, secretly cut his head with a razor blade he had hidden in his glove, and his team refused to continue; Brazil were eventually awarded a 2-0 win and Chile were banned from the 1994 tournament. A 2-0 win over Malta on **15th November** sealed the Republic of Ireland's first ever qualification for the finals. Luciano Pavarotti was the star guest at the draw for the finals in Rome on **9th December**; the tenor's recording of the aria 'Nessun Dorma' was used as the BBC's World Cup theme tune and went to Number Two in the charts. The opening game of Italia' 90 on **8th June 1990** provided a shock when François Omam-Biyik's goal earned a 1-0 victory for Cameroon over holders Argentina. When Nery Pumpido broke his leg in Argentina's 2-0 win over the Soviet Union on **13th June**, Sergio Goycochea took his place and went on to become his country's player of the tournament. West Germany's victory over England on **4th July** was the eighth out of the 14 knockout matches to be decided on penalties or after extra time. On **8th July**, Argentina's Pedro Monzón became the first player to be sent off in a World Cup final; he was joined by team-mate Gustavo Dezotti 22 minutes later. After a month of largely disappointing football, the goal average per game was 2.2 – the lowest in World Cup history.

ABOVE: Defender Terry Butcher bled for his country in the 0-0 qualifying draw with Sweden in September 1989.

BELOW: On the eve of England's departure for the finals, controversial news leaked out that manager Bobby Robson (pictured with then FA Chief Executive Graham Kelly) would not have his contract renewed after the finals.

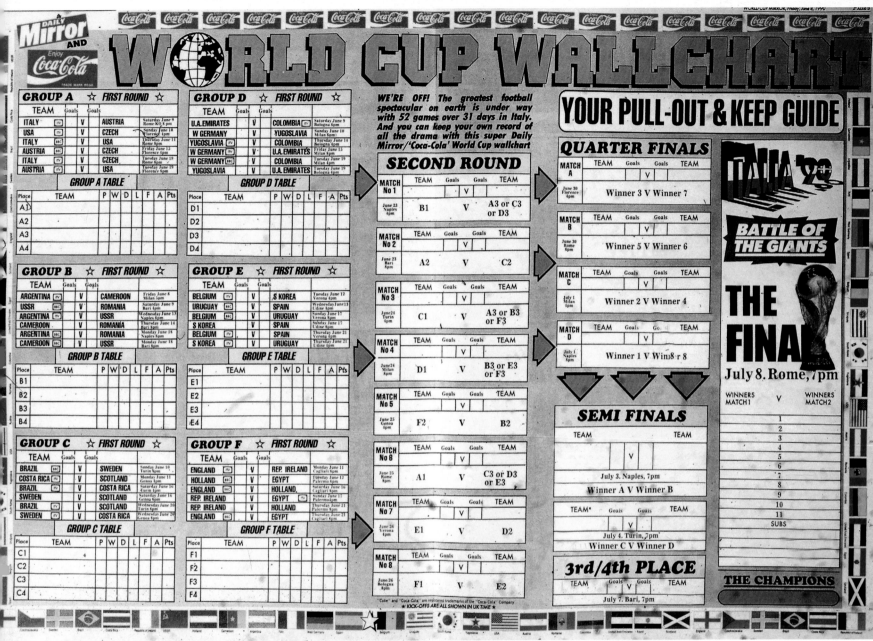

LEFT: Ally McCoist (centre) helped Scotland book their fifth consecutive appearance in the finals, overcoming France in a tough qualifying group and despite losing 3-0 to the French in October 1989.

The Fading Flowers of Scotland

For the fifth tournament in succession, Scotland qualified for the finals – a remarkable achievement for a nation of just 5 million people – but yet again the team failed to progress beyond the opening group stage. Confidence had been high, especially after a 1-0 warm-up win against Argentina, but when it mattered for real, the Scots reverted to some familiar failings.

RIGHT: Head bowed with disappointment, Gordon Durie summed up another frustrating tournament for Scotland.

BELOW: Despite goalkeeper Jim Leighton ending all ends up, Scotland rallied with a merited 2-1 win over Sweden in Genoa. Just as in previous World Cups, this meant that Scotland went into the final group game needing a heroic but unlikely victory to make it through to the next phase.

ABOVE: A recurring feature of Scottish World Cup campaigns has been for the side to suffer embarrassing results, and 1990 was no exception. The 1-0 loss to tiny Costa Rica, with Juan Arnoldo Cayasso (above) scoring the winning goal, ranks among one of Scotland's most infamous results.

LEFT: Manager Andy Roxburgh and his successor Craig Brown saw goals from Stuart McCall and a Mo Johnston penalty as justified reward for the team's resilience.

ABOVE: Needing a win in the final Group C game if other results were not in their favour, Scotland faced a Brazil side that, while it was a pale imitation of previous *Seleção*, still presented an ominous obstacle to Scottish hopes. For 81 minutes the dream was a possibility until the otherwise excellent Leighton could only parry Alemao's long-range shot. While Leighton and Gary Gillespie managed to squirm the loose ball away from Careca, Müller was on hand to follow up and dash Scottish hopes in cruel fashion.

LEFT & RIGHT: For two Scots football fans, Italia '90

189

Luck of the Irish

The Republic of Ireland enjoyed an altogether happier tournament on their World Cup debut.

The team may have been managed by an English World Cup winner, and staffed with players who had varying degrees of Celtic lineage, but few other sides played with as much pride in the shirt as Ireland. Lining up for the quarter-final game against Italy were, left to right, back row: Kevin Moran, Paul McGrath, Pat Bonner, Mick McCarthy, Andy Townsend, Steve Staunton. Front row: John Aldridge, Niall Quinn, Kevin Sheedy, Chris Morris, Ray Houghton.

LEFT: When in Rome... Jack Charlton became a national hero on the western side of the Irish Sea off the back of his colourful exploits with the Republic's team. His avuncular style and refusal to bow to the reputations of more illustrious opponents inspired the team to an unlikely quarter-final meeting with the hosts in the Italian capital.

RIGHT: The opening 1-1 draw with England may have been short on entertainment, but it showed how Ireland could compete with the supposed big guns.

190

ABOVE: Next up were Egypt, making their first appearance in the finals since 1934. The game ended goalless, but another draw with the Netherlands ensured Ireland's passage to the last 16. Their penalty shoot-out victory over the highly rated Romania, sealed with Bonners' brilliant save from Daniel Timofte and David O'Leary's nerveless spot kick, maintained Irish interest into the fourth week of the competition.

LEFT & ABOVE: The fairytale came to an end with defeat by a single goal, scored by Salvatore "Totò" Schillaci (left). The Italian striker was one of the emblematic figures of the tournament, winning the Golden Boot with six goals and his bug-eyed, fist-pumping celebrations providing some much-needed passion in an event otherwise curiously lacking in genuine drama. His team-mate Roberto Baggio (above) briefly flickered into life, a brilliant solo effort against Czechoslovakia giving an all-too-isolated illustration of his undoubted talent.

England on Song

England's progression through the tournament was something of a surprise. With a beleaguered manager harangued by the media and on his way out of the job, Bryan Robson yet again injured, and a squad full of players who had failed to live up to expectations in previous tournaments, relatively little was expected of the team when compared with the hype of previous campaigns. This reflected a generally weary attitude towards the national game that seems almost inconceivable when viewed from the modern era, as the sport is now all-pervasive in its popularity. In 1990 the European club ban that had followed the Heysel disaster five years earlier had left English football tactically backward, its infrastructure tired, inferior and unsafe; Italy's sparkling new World Cup stadiums shamed the dilapidated condition of English grounds, and symbolized the gulf between the respective football cultures.

And yet there were signs the English game was on the way back. Attendances had started to tentatively increase; hooliganism was in decline; and the national team was relatively settled and balanced, with what proved to be a neat blend of experience and youthful enterprise. The fact that New Order, one of the most avant-garde of British pop bands, had got into the studio to record England's official World Cup song (right), was an indicator that football was once again something people wanted to identify with.

ABOVE: Hooliganism, particularly of the depressingly jingoistic kind, was still a problem, and trouble broke out before and after the game against the Dutch in Cagliari. But the behaviour of fans was not as bad as feared and led to the lifting of the European ban on British clubs.

BELOW: The picture that began to emerge from Italia '90 was an altogether happier one, embodied in the jovial form of Paul Gascoigne, who for once (below) was on the receiving end of a practical joke from England team-mates.

After the draw with Ireland, England drew a blank in a goalless game with the Netherlands. The Dutch, reigning European Champions and fielding the Milan trio of Frank Rijkaard, Marco van Basten and Ruud Gullit, (right, challenged by Des Walker), were strongly tipped for success on their return to the finals after a 12-year absence, but stuttered and went out in the first round. England, by contrast, went from strength to strength. Mark Wright was introduced as sweeper and he and the team clicked with his goal in a 1-0 win over Egypt, ensuring England's passage through to the last 16.

RIGHT: The last-16 tie against Belgium was a stalemate and heading towards penalties before the dramatic intervention of substitute David Platt. A powerful run from Gascoigne won England a free-kick in the 119th minute, which the Tottenham midfielder clipped into the Belgium area. Platt acrobatically turned and volleyed the ball into the net to give England a place in the quarter-finals.

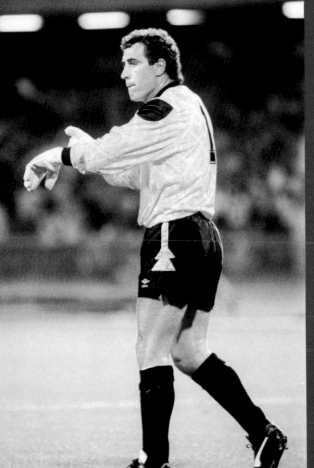

ABOVE: England met Cameroon in the quarter-finals but if they were expecting an easy ride they were to be rudely disappointed. The West African side took a 2-1 lead with just 25 minutes to go in the second half, and only a brace of penalties enabled England to go through.

LEFT: Peter Shilton, making his 123rd England appearance, wasn't quite calling for time on his international career but reminding referee Mendez to blow the final whistle. By the end of Italia '90, the veteran keeper had set an England record of 125 caps.

RIGHT: Exhausted but happy, goalscorers Platt and Lineker celebrate a hard-earned victory. West Germany awaited in the semi-final.

Lions' Pride

Cameroon's outstanding display in 1990 confirmed what many pundits had long predicted: African teams were no longer an exotic curiosity to be patronized, but a genuine force to be reckoned with. "The Indomitable Lions" helped pave the way for a succession of teams from the African continent, and Cameroon qualified to compete in South Africa 2010 along with five other African sides.

> *We didn't underestimate them. They were a lot better than we thought.*
>
> Bobby Robson

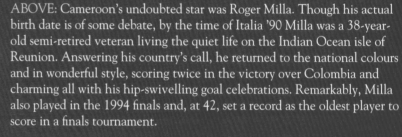

ABOVE: Cameroon's undoubted star was Roger Milla. Though his actual birth date is of some debate, by the time of Italia '90 Milla was a 38-year-old semi-retired veteran living the quiet life on the Indian Ocean isle of Reunion. Answering his country's call, he returned to the national colours and in wonderful style, scoring twice in the victory over Colombia and charming all with his hip-swivelling goal celebrations. Remarkably, Milla also played in the 1994 finals and, at 42, set a record as the oldest player to score in a finals tournament.

LEFT: World Cup 1990 quarter-final: England 3, Cameroon 2. Cameroon goalscorer Emmanuel Kunde celebrates his equalizing goal against England in Naples.

BELOW: The defeated side take a well-deserved lap of honour.

–STAR–
OF THE TOURNAMENT

Paul Gascoigne

It is difficult to overestimate the impact Paul Gascoigne had on football with his World Cup finals performances. Though he only played in six games (long-term injury and lack of form meant 1990 was his sole tournament), he played a major part in lifting the English game out of the doldrums with his skilful, all-action displays that so nearly brought England glory, encapsulated in the epic semi-final defeat to West Germany. At the same time, his effervescent, madcap personality blew away decades of stuffy convention and the implicit perception that English players were passive underachievers who knew their place. True success is still to elude the national side, but Gascoigne's example raised standards, injected a sense of pride back into supporting the national team, and, for a while at least, reinvigorated belief that the country could replicate the victory of 1966.

No respecter of reputation, Gascoigne could battle with the best including West Germany's captain Lothar Matthäus.

FOOTBALL –STATS–

Paul Gascoigne

Name: Paul John Gascoigne

Born: 1967

International Playing Career: 1988-1998

International Appearances: 57

Goals: 10

The incident when Gazza's World Cup dream effectively ended, but also the moment that won him the nation's affections. Nine minutes into extra time, after the sides have fought out a thrilling 1-1 draw, Gascoigne's mistimed though hardly malicious tackle on Thomas Berthold (and the German defender's theatrical reaction) earned Gascoigne a booking from ref José Ramiz Wright, and with it a suspension that would rule him out of the final. The tears soon followed.

197

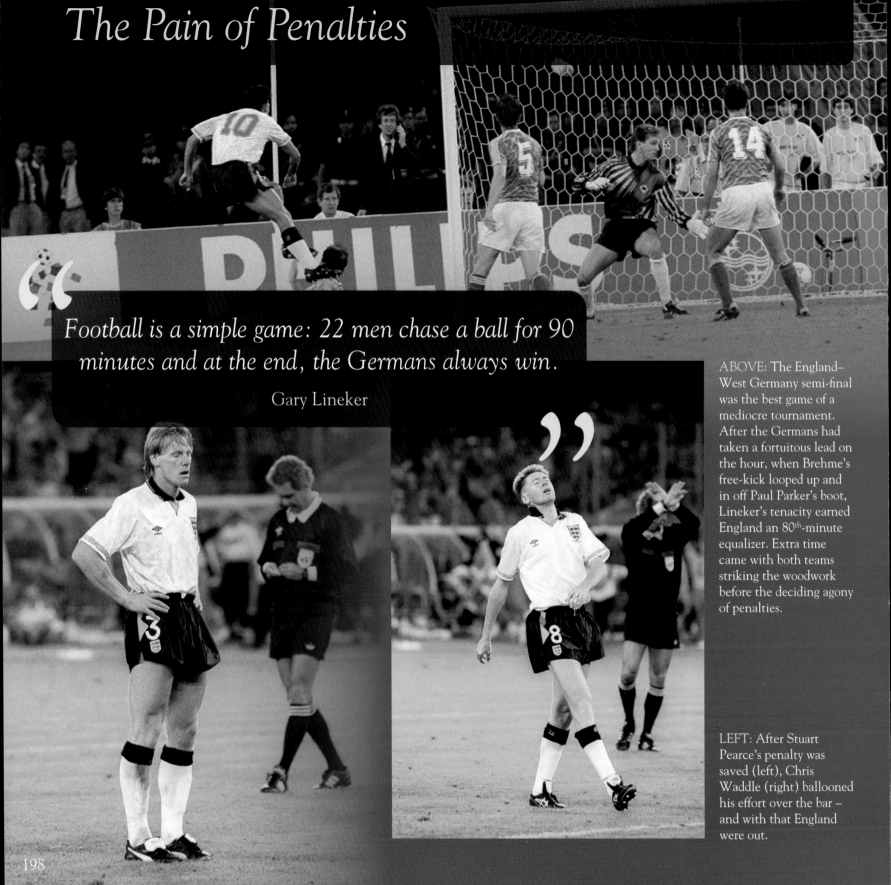

The Pain of Penalties

> Football is a simple game: 22 men chase a ball for 90 minutes and at the end, the Germans always win.

Gary Lineker

ABOVE: The England–West Germany semi-final was the best game of a mediocre tournament. After the Germans had taken a fortuitous lead on the hour, when Brehme's free-kick looped up and in off Paul Parker's boot, Lineker's tenacity earned England an 80th-minute equalizer. Extra time came with both teams striking the woodwork before the deciding agony of penalties.

LEFT: After Stuart Pearce's penalty was saved (left), Chris Waddle (right) ballooned his effort over the bar – and with that England were out.

ABOVE LEFT: Terry Butcher comforts Gascoigne.

ABOVE RIGHT: The despair of the defeated footballer.

LEFT: Back home in a Manchester pub, young and old shared in the agony of defeat.

The England team arrived back home to an unexpectedly tumultuous reception, as Gascoigne played to the gallery with a pair of comedy breasts. A smile was back on the face of English football.

UEFA to lift ban

By IAN GIBB

ENGLISH football clubs are poised to step back into European competitions next season.

Sports minister Colin Moynihan is likely to recommend to UEFA tomorrow that the five-year ban imposed after the Heysel disaster of 1985 should now be lifted following the relatively good behaviour of England fans in Italy.

Moynihan remained tight-lipped yesterday as he prepared his report for UEFA.

But Government sources have indicated that he will advise that the ban should be lifted, at least on a trial basis.

If Moynihan's report is positive, then UEFA is likely to go along with it – and Aston Villa would take their place in next season's UEFA Cup, with Manchester United in the Cup-winners' Cup.

Champions Liverpool, however, must still wait to learn their fate. They were intended to serve a further three years once the indefinite ban was

MOYNIHAN: Ready

lifted and must now hope for an amnesty for the season after next.

Moynihan said yesterday: "We are still working on the report. Further reports will come through in the next 48 hours, so we will be in a position to report to UEFA on Tuesday."

New hope for the clubs followed remarks on Saturday by the English police chief who helped the Italian police at the World Cup.

Assistant Chief Constable Malcolm George, of Greater Manchester police, praised the "tremendous success" of the anti-hooligan operation at the World Cup.

"If English police were asked to assist a host country, then I feel that we could safely go into Europe," he said.

WE T

NEWS+NEW

Nige

NIGEL MAN the end of Ferrari blowi

Mansell's F notched up h hat-trick in B controlled ra

BELOW: The contrast between England's homecoming and the 1990 final was stark. Argentina had beaten Italy in the semi-final on penalties in Naples where Maradona had been idolized during his time in the Italian league. The football world turned on him and his side in the final itself, however, where their cynical approach led to two dismissals and made West Germany unlikely favourites amongst neutrals. A grim game was settled five minutes from time when Sensini fouled Voller, and Brehme scored from the spot – an outcome entirely in keeping with the tournament.

T GERMANY 1

ARGENTINA 0

WORLD CUP SPECIAL

E GAME

THAT DIED OF SHAME

We are champs of fair play!

Brehme sinks Argies

DIEGO Maradona shed tears of sadness and shame as his glittering World Cup career crashed in disgrace here last night.

Maradona's grief at losing his world crown to West Germany was flashed upon the giant screens in the Olympic Stadium, as he wept just a yard from the golden trophy.

But the little Argentinian skipper, booed and jeered by the crowd, could not get his Hand of God anywhere near it.

Argentina finished with nine men and their manager Carlos Bilardo had rushed to the field to pull his snarling players from Mexican referee Edgardo Codesal Mendes.

Cynical

When the referee sent off a second Argentinian, Gustavo Desotti, they rushed to Mendes with such force that they shoved and pushed him until he raised the yellow card in the face of Maradona.

Dirty Diego and his cynical team had disfigured soccer's showpiece – and this final will forever be remembered for its brutality and not its brilliance.

Argentina had been reduced to ten men in the 67th minute when Pedro Monzon, a second half substitute, was dismissed for a vicious lunge on Jurgen Klinsmann.

But that was just the prelude to Argentina's shameful behaviour.

Nasty Argie bargy

OUCH! German Guido Buchwald is fouled by Argentina's Oscar Ruggeri in another unseemly clash.

South American tempers boiled over five minutes from the end when West Germany's shining star Lothar Matthaeus split the defence to find Rudi Voeller, who was brought down by Roberto Sensini.

Despairing

Maradona rushed to the referee almost begging him not to give a penalty and there was a yellow card for Juan Simon for continuing his arguments.

Full back Andy Brehme plunged his spot-kick deep into the corner of the net past the despairing dive of keeper Sergio Goycoechea.

Once the passionate celebrations of the German players had subsided, Jurgen Kohler kept hold of the ball as he wasted time in the corner.

Desotti grabbed Kohler by the scruff of

the neck, spun him round and sent him crashing to the ground.

The retaliation got what it deserved - another red card for Argentina.

Now the Mexican referee was jostled and abused by the Argentinians in the some of the most disgraceful scenes ever seen in a World Cup final - and Maradona was shown the yellow card for arguing.

At the final whistle with the German celebrations ringing round the stadium, Maradona's pitiful crouching figure appeared on the big screens - a sight that brought jeers from the crowd.

Maradona had vowed to bow out of World Cup competition in glory.

Instead, he ran into a

solid German brick wall named Guido Buchwald.

Maradona was given no room to ignite Argentina as Buchwald restricted him to just three touches in the first ten minutes, one header and two back passes.

Dominance

Such was his dominance that Buchwald had the audacity to break forward himself, taking the ball off Maradona's toes to storm down the right wing but his cross was just too long for Voeller.

When Buchwald made a tackle that sent Maradona dramatically flying, Pierre Littbarski

tapped him on the shoulder suggesting he got up and stopped over-acting.

But there was genuine pain for Maradona when he was crushed between Voeller and Buchwald, and Voeller paid the price with a yellow card for stepping on Maradona during a rare occasion when he looked capable of wriggling free.

Otherwise, Mara-

TEARS: Maradona is consoled by trainer Echavarria

HARRY HARRIS reports from Rome

JUST CHAMPION

WUNDERBAR! West German skipper Lothar Matthaeus holds the World Cup aloft after Andy Brehme's late penalty sunk a shameful Argentina 1-0.

dona's only contributions was when he put through a superb pass for Desotti to chase, and a free kick on the edge of the box that he hit over the bar.

In contrast, his opposite number Matthaeus was the man who ran the match.

Matthaeus conjured a defence-splitting pass, searching out sweeper Klaus Augenthaler who

was brought down by the keeper, but the referee turned down German claims for a penalty.

Once Monzon was sent off it seemed only a matter of time before West Germany would eventually break through.

It was a minor miracle that Argentina held out for so long, even with 11 players.

The Germans gained revenge for their World Cup final defeat four years ago in Mexico when there was a vastly different Maradona in the Azteca stadium.

But last night he was just a shadow of the man who destroyed West Germany in the Azteca stadium.

He was a sad little figure, but the world won't cry for Argentina or for Maradona.

"Codesal was scared of getting to a penalty shoot-out, West Germany were falling away," he said.

ENGLAND

ENGLAND manager Bobby Robson and star striker Gary Lineker did not leave Italy empty-handed at the end of the World Cup after all.

Despite the eventual disappoinment of finishing fourth in the finals, Robson and Lineker still found themselves on the winner's rostrum last night in Rome after the Argentina-West Germany final.

They were there to pick up England's award as the tournament's 'fair play' champions, a prize awarded to the team with the best disciplinary record in the tournament.

During the seven matches of the tournament, England received just five bookings and conceded a total of 106 fouls.

After seeing a niggling match, with two Argentine players sent off, Lineker said: "We have the most honest footballers in the world.

"We don't roll around pretending we are injured. We don't play-act with referees. We play a hard, fair game and this award proves it.

"It shows we have got players with the right attitude. You get none of the antics we have seen in the final tonight."

Robson, who is stepping down to become manager of Dutch club PSV Eindhoven, said: "At least we have won something. We have made a lot of friends here and restored our reputation.

"I must admit we were a bit envious tonight after we had come so close. We were two missed penalty kicks away from the final.

"We feel we could have played well enough to have beaten Argentina."

Diego's disgrace

➡ **From back page**

trouble controlling his team. He said: "I tried to calm them down. Some players lost their cool. They got upset.

"I don't want to talk about referees, and I'm not going to protest to FIFA about this one."

But Maradona said the penalty was awarded to "make the Italians, them (FIFA) and everybody happy. There was something fishy."

Argentina came so entrenched in defence, they had just one shot on goal. Although the penalty was a bad decision few would begrudge West Germany their victory.

They tried to go forward and get their reward when Rudi Voeller was pulled down by Roberto Sensini who clearly played the ball and Andy Brehme coolly slotted home the penalty.

Maradona thought Argentina should have had a penalty when Calderon tumbled in the penalty area.

NEWS+NEWS+NEWS+NEWS

sfires

eight laps from Prix with his oke.

ate Alain Prost Prix win and a with a typically

Martin fires

New Zealand 14, Gt Britain 16

MARTIN OFFIAH ended his scoring famine in style to leave the Lions feasting on their first overseas Test series victory for 11 years. He finished off an 80-yard move with seven minutes of the second Test remaining - and with the tourists trailing by two points.

201

The Marketing Game
1994

Knighted in World Cup year, Bobby Charlton perches on the knee of USA Mascot "Striker".

On **4**th **July 1988,** American Independence Day, FIFA president João Havelange announced that the USA would host the 15th World Cup, seeing off rival bids from Morocco and Brazil. Fulfilling the commitment to have a professional league in exchange for hosting the World Cup, US football authorities set up the Major Soccer League in **1993.** The league did not start until **1996.** With the conclusion of European preliminary games on **17**th **November 1993** the state of Russia (and not the Soviet Union) qualified for the first time; a unified Germany competed for the first time since 1938. During the opening ceremony on **17**th **June 1994,** Diana Ross missed a staged penalty. The 1-1 draw between USA and Switzerland on **18**th **June** at the Pontiac Silverdome in Detroit was the first World Cup finals game to be played indoors. On the same day Ireland beat Italy 1-0. Colombia's Andres Escobar scored an own goal in the 2-1 defeat by the US on **22**nd **June;** a little over a week later he was murdered back home in Colombia by a gunman who was reported to have said "thanks for the own goal" before shooting Escobar dead. After the 2-1 win over Nigeria on **25**th **June,** Argentina's Diego Maradona failed a drugs test. Russia's Oleg Salenko set a new record by scoring five goals in the 6-1 thrashing of Cameroon on **28**th **June.** Germany missed out on a fourth successive World Cup final after losing 2-1 to Bulgaria in the quarter-final on **10**th **July.** Brazil won their fourth World Cup and their first since 1970 with a penalty shoot-out victory over Italy on **17**th **July.**

Group A	Group B	Group C
USA Switzerland Colombia Romania	Brazil Russia Cameroon Sweden	Germany Bolivia Spain South Korea

Sat June 18
Detroit:
USA v Switzerland (4.30pm)
Los Angeles:
Colombia v Romania (Midnight.30)

Wed June 22
Detroit:
Romania v Switzerland (9pm)
Los Angeles:
USA v Colombia (Midnight.30)

Sun June 26
Los Angeles:
USA v Romania (9pm)
San Francisco:
Switzerland v Colombia (9pm)

Sun June 19
Los Angeles:
Cameroon v Sweden (Midnight.30)

Mon June 20
San Francisco:
Brazil v Russia (9pm)

Fri June 24
San Francisco:
Brazil v Cameroon (9pm)
Detroit:
Sweden v Russia (Midnight.30)

Tue June 28
San Francisco:
Russia v Cameroon (9pm)
Detroit:
Brazil v Sweden (9pm)

Fri June 17
Chicago:
Germany v Bolivia (8pm)
Dallas:
Spain v South Korea (12.30pm)

Tue June 21
Chicago:
Germany v Spain (9pm)

Thu June 23
Boston:
South Korea v Bolivia (Midnight.30)

Mon June 27
Chicago:
Bolivia v Spain (9pm)
Dallas:
Germany v South Korea (9pm)

Group D	Group E	Group F
Argentina Greece Nigeria Bulgaria	Italy Rep of Ireland Norway Mexico	Belgium Morocco Holland Saudi Arabia

Tue June 21
Boston:
Argentina v Greece (5.30pm)
Dallas:
Nigeria v Bulgaria (12.30pm)

Sat June 25
Boston:
Argentina v Nigeria (9pm)

Sun June 26
Chicago:
Bulgaria v Greece (5.30pm)

Thu June 30
Boston:
Greece v Nigeria (Midnight.30)
Dallas:
Argentina v Bulgaria (Midnight.30)

Sat June 18
New York:
Italy v Ireland (9pm)

Sun June 19
Washington:
Norway v Mexico (9pm)

Thu June 23
New York:
Italy v Norway (9pm)

Fri June 24
Orlando:
Mexico v Ireland (5.30pm)

Tue June 28
New York:
Ireland v Norway (5.30pm)
Washington:
Italy v Mexico (5.30pm)

Sun June 19
Orlando:
Belgium v Morocco (5.30pm)

Mon June 20
Washington:
Holland v Saudi Arabia (Midnight.30)

Sat June 25
New York:
Saudi Arabia v Morocco (5.30pm)
Orlando:
Belgium v Holland (5.30pm)

Wed June 29
Orlando:
Morocco v Holland (5.30pm)
Washington:
Belgium v Saudi Arabia (5.30pm)

John Barnes warmed up for a qualifying match against Turkey in April 1993. The England scarf was not required for the finals.

Did he not like that... All the hope for English football engendered by Italia '90 quickly dissipated into regression on the pitch and rampant commercialization off it. The establishment of the Premier League in 1992 dragged the domestic game into the modern age, transformed stadiums, led to a boom in attendances and made English league football the most monied in the world – but of what benefit to the national side? Graham Taylor's team failed to qualify for the 1994 finals, and despite the promises that England would once again rule the world, the national team had not progressed beyond the quarter-finals up to the 2010 tournament.

A 2-0 defeat away to the Netherlands ended England's 1994 qualifying campaign. Taylor was mercilessly pilloried by the media, and was soon out of what had become known as "the impossible job". Left to right: Phil Neal, Taylor, Lawrie McMenemy and veteran of the 1970 World Cup, Peter Bonetti.

LEFT: Ronald Koeman's free-kick goal, moments after he should have been sent off for a professional foul, was symptomatic of Taylor's unfortunate reign.

Brazil striker Romario may have been the star of the tournament, but the *Mirror*'s writers were in no doubt as to the true value of a very modern World Cup: in Harry Harris' phrase it was all about the "till, turnstiles and television". Yet, the final excepted, many of the games were exciting, with plenty of goals and huge crowds. The total of 141 goals was the highest since 1982 while the average attendance of 68,991 is still a World Cup record.

There was no doubting the passion of these Brazilian ex-pats celebrating in London, but the World Cup now had the unmistakable air of a money-making exercise as opposed to a competition purely about the football. Commercial interests had always been a part of the tournament, but the degree to which each team and player had become a marketable commodity meant the World Cup would never quite feel the same again.

Acknowledgments

Selected sources:
Daily Mirror
FIFA.com
BBC
Englandfootballonline
Rsssf.com
The Book of Football Quotations, Phil Shaw (Ebury 2003)
Alan Mullery – The Autobiography, Alan Mullery (Headline 2006)
History of the World Cup, Michael Archer (Hamlyn 1978)
Ossie, Osvaldo Ardiles (Bantam 2009)

Thanks to all at Mirrorpix: Vito, Manjit, Dave, John, Alex, Fergus, and Mel, plus
Richard Havers, Paul Moreton, Troy Hagan, Martin Cloake, Kevin Gardner and all at Haynes.

Special thanks to all the photographers, without whom...